The Life of Prayer
and
The Power of Stillness

The Life
of Prayer

AND

The Power
of Stillness

A. B. SIMPSON

SCOTTS VALLEY
CALIFORNIA
2010

The Life of Prayer and The Power of Stillness

A. B. Simpson (1843–1919)

Copyright © Albert Benjamin Simpson 1890

ISBN 9781453858790

Contents

THE LIFE OF PRAYER

Introduction

THE LIFE OF PRAYER—great and sacred theme! It leads us into the Holy of Holies and the secret place of the Most High. It is the very life of the Christian, and it touches the life of God Himself.

We enter the sacred chamber on our knees. We still our thoughts and words, and say: "Lord, teach us to pray. Give us Thy holy desires, and let our prayer be the very echo of Thy will. Give us Thy Spirit as our Advocate within. Open our eyes to see our Great High Priest and Advocate above, and help us so to abide in Him, and to have His Word so abiding in us, that we shall ask what we will, and it shall be done unto us." And as in ignorance and weakness we venture to speak and think upon this vital theme, "Let the words of my mouth, and the meditation of my heart, be acceptable in thy sight, O Lord, my strength, and my redeemer." And may every true word and thought of this little volume be a living experience to him who speaks and to all who hear, and so minister to the life of prayer in all our lives, that it shall bring, in some humble measure, an answer to the greatest of all prayers, and the prayer with which this opening chapter begins and to which this book is dedicated, "Our Father which art in heaven, Hallowed be thy name."

—A. B. SIMPSON

~ 1 ~

The Pattern Prayer

"And he said unto them, When ye pray, say, Our Father which art in heaven, Hallowed be thy name. Thy kingdom come. Thy will be done, as in heaven, so in earth. Give us day by day our daily bread. And forgive us our sins; for we also forgive every one that is indebted to us. And lead us not into temptation; but deliver us from evil" (Luke 11:2–4).

THIS WONDERFUL PRAYER was dictated by our Lord in reply to the question on the part of His disciples, "Lord, teach us to pray." His answer was to bid them pray. This is the only way we shall ever learn to pray, by just beginning to do it. And as the babbling child learns the art of speech by speaking, and the lark mounts up to the heights of the sky by beating its little wings again and again upon the air, so prayer will teach us how to pray; and the more we pray, the more shall we learn the mysteries and heights and depths of prayer. And the more we pray, the more we shall realize the incomparable fullness and completeness of this unequaled prayer, the prayer of universal Christendom, the common liturgy of the Church of God, the earliest and holiest recollection of every Christian child, and the latest utterance often of the departing soul. We who have used it most have come to feel that there is no want which it does not interpret and no holy aspiration which it may not express. There is nothing else in the Holy Scriptures which more fully evolves the great principles that underlie the divine philosophy of prayer.

It teaches us that all true prayer begins in the recognition of the Father. It is not the cry of nature to an unknown God, but the intelligent converse of a child with his heavenly Father. It presupposes that the suppliant has become a child, and it assumes that the mediation of the Son has preceded the revelation of the Father. No one, therefore, can truly pray until he has accepted the Lord Jesus Christ as Savior and received through Him the child-heart in regeneration, and then been led into the realization of sonship in the family of God. The Person to whom prayer is directly addressed is the Father as distinguished from the Son and the Holy Spirit. The great purpose of Christ's mediation is to bring us to God and reveal to us the Father as our Father in reconciliation and fellowship. It is not wrong to address the Son and Spirit in our hearts. The name suggests the spirit of confidence, and this is essential to prayer.

The first view given of God in the Lord's Prayer is not His majesty but His paternal love. To the listening disciples, this must have been a strange expression from the lips of their Lord as a pattern for them. Never had Jewish ear heard God so named, at least in His relation to the individual. "The Father of the Nation" He was sometimes called, but no sinful man had ever dared to call God his Father. They, doubtless, had heard their Master speak in this delightful name of God as His Father, but that they should call Jehovah by such a name had never dawned upon their legal and unillumined minds. And yet it really means that we may and should recognize that God is our Father in the very sense in which He is His Father, and ours as partakers of His Sonship and His Name. The Name expresses the most personal and tender love, protection, care, and intimacy; and it gives to prayer, at the very outset, the beautiful atmosphere of the home circle and the delightful affectionate and intimate fellowship of friend with friend.

Beloved, have you thus learned to pray? Do wondering angels look down upon your closet every day to see a humble and sinful creature of the dust talking to the majestic Sovereign of the skies, as an infant lies upon its mother's breast or prattles without a fear upon her knee?

Can it be said to you, "I write unto you, little children, because ye have known the Father"?

It teaches us that prayer should recognize the majesty and almightiness of God. The words "who art in heaven," or rather "in the heavens," are intended to give to the conception of the Divine Being a very definite and local personality. He is not a vague influence or pantheistic presence, but a distinct Person, exalted above matter and nature and having local habitation, to which the mind is directed, and where He occupies the throne of actual sovereignty over all the universe. He is also recognized as above our standpoint and level, in the heavens, higher than our little world, and exalted above all other elements and forces that need His controlling power. It enthrones Him in the place of highest power, authority and glory.

And so true prayer must ever recognize at once the nearness and greatness of God. The Old Testament, therefore, is full of the sublimest representation of the majesty of God, and the more fully we realize His greatness, the more boldly will we dare to claim His interposition in prayer in all our trials and emergencies.

Beloved, have we learned, as we bow the knee in prayer, that we are talking with Him Who still says to us as to Abraham, "I am El Shaddai, the Almighty God"; to Jeremiah, "I am the Lord, the God of all flesh: is there any thing too hard for me?"; to Isaiah, "Hast thou not known? Hast thou not heard, that the everlasting God, the Lord, the Creator of the ends of the earth, fainteth not, neither is weary? There is no searching of his understanding."

It teaches us that prayer is not only a fellowship with God but a fellowship of human hearts. "Our Father" lifts each of us at once out of ourselves, and, if nowhere else on earth, at least at the throne of grace, makes us members one of another. Of course, it is assumed that the first link in the fellowship is Christ, our Elder Brother, and so there is no single heart, however isolated, but that may come with this prayer with perfect truthfulness, and hand in hand with Christ say, "Christ's and mine." But, undoubtedly, it chiefly refers to the fellowship of human hearts. The highest promises made to prayer are those who agree, or, as the Greek more beautifully expresses it, "symphonize" on earth. There is no place where we can love our friends so beautifully or so purely as at the throne of grace. There is no exercise in which the differences of Christians melt away as when their hearts meet together in the unity of prayer, and there is no remedy for the divisions of Christianity but to come closer to the Father, and then, perforce, we shall be in touch with each other.

It teaches us that worship is the highest element in prayer. "Hallowed be thy name" is more than any petition of the Lord's Prayer. It brings us directly to God Himself and makes His glory supreme, above all our thoughts and all our wants. It reminds us that the first purpose of our prayers should ever be, not the supply of our personal needs, but the worship and adoration of our God. In the ancient feasts, everything was first brought to Him, and then it was given to the worshiper in several cases for his use, and its use was hallowed by the fact that it had already been laid at Jehovah's feet. And so the spirit that can truly utter this prayer and fully enter into its meaning can receive all the other petitions of it with double blessing. Not until we have first become satisfied with God Himself and realize that His glory is above all our desires and interests are we prepared to receive any blessing in the highest sense; and when we can truly say, "Hallowed be thy name, whatever comes to me," we have the substance of all blessing in our heart.

This is the innermost chamber of the Holy of Holies, and none can enter it without becoming conscious of the hallowing blessing that falls upon and fills us with the glory which we have ascribed to Him. The sacred sense of His overshadowing, the deep and penetrating solemnity, the heavenly calm that fills the heart which can truly utter these sacred words, constitute a blessing above all other blessings that even this prayer can ask.

Beloved, have we learned to begin our prayer in this holy place, on this heavenly plane? Then, indeed, have we learned to pray.

It teaches us that true prayer recognizes the establishment of the Kingdom of God as the chief purpose of the divine will and the supreme desire of every true Christian. More than our own temporal or even spiritual needs are we to pray for the establishment of that

Kingdom. This implies that the real remedy for all that needs prayer is the restoration of the Kingdom of God. The true cause of all human trouble is that men are out of the divine order and the world is in rebellion against its rightful Sovereign, and not until that Kingdom is reestablished in every heart and in all the world can the blessings which prayer desires be realized. Of course, it includes in a primary sense the establishment of the Kingdom of God in the individual heart, but much more in the world at large, in fulfillment of God's great purpose of redemption. It is, in short, the prayer for the accomplishment of redemption and its glorious consummation in the coming of our Lord and the setting up of His Millennial Kingdom. What an exalted view this gives of prayer! How it raises us above our petty selfish cares and cries! It is said of a devoted minister, Dr. Backus of Baltimore, that when told he was dying and had only half an hour to live, he asked them to raise him from his bed and place him upon his knees, and he spent the last half hour of his life in one ceaseless prayer for the evangelization of the world. Truly that was a glorious place to end a life of prayer! But the Lord's Prayer begins with this lofty theme and teaches us that it should ever be the first concern and petition of every loyal subject of the Redeemer's Kingdom.

Must it not be true, beloved, that the failure of many of our prayers may be traced to their selfishness, and the innumerable efforts we have spent upon our own interests, and the little we have ever asked for the Kingdom of our Lord? There is no blessing so great as that which comes when our hearts are lifted out of self and become one with Christ in intercession for others and for His cause. There is no joy so pure as that of taking the burden of our Master's cause on our hearts and bearing it with Him every day in ceaseless prayer, as though its interests wholly depended upon the uplifting of our hands and the remembrance of our faith. "Prayer shall be made for him continually," is one of the promises respecting our blessed Lord.

Beloved, have we prayed for Jesus as much as we have for ourselves? There is no ministry which will bring more power and blessing upon the world and from which we ourselves will reap larger harvests of eternal fruit than the habit of believing, definite, and persistent prayer for the progress of Christ's Kingdom, for the needs of His church and work, for His ministers and servants, and especially for the evangelization of the world and the vast neglected myriads who know not how to pray for themselves. Oh, let us awaken from our spiritual selfishness and learn the meaning of the petition "Thy kingdom come!"

It teaches us that true prayer is founded upon the will of God as its limitation and encouragement. It is not asking for things because we want them, for the primary condition of all true prayer is the renunciation of our own will that we may desire and receive God's will instead. But having done this, and recognizing the will of our Father as the standard of our desires and petitions, we are to claim these petitions when they are in accordance with His will with a force and tenacity as great as the will of God itself. And so this petition, instead of being a limitation of prayer, is really a confirmation of our faith and gives us the right to claim that the petition thus conformed to His will shall be imperatively fulfilled. Therefore, there is no prayer so mighty, so sure, so full of blessing, as this little sentence at which so many of us have often trembled: "Thy will be done." It is not the death-knell of all our happiness but the pledge of all possible blessing; for if it is the will of God to bless us, we shall be blessed. Happy are they who suspend their desires until they know their Father's will, and then, asking according to His will, they can rise to the height of His own mighty promise, "If ye abide in me, and my words abide in you, ye shall ask what ye will, and it shall be done unto you." "Thus saith the Lord . . . ask me of things to come concerning my sons, and concerning the work of my hands command ye me." What more can we ask of ourselves and others than that God's highest will, and that for us, shall be fulfilled?

How shall we know that will? At the very least, we may always know it by His Word and promise, and we may be very sure we are not transcending its infinite bounds if we ask anything that is covered by a promise of His Holy Word, but we may immediately turn that promise into an order on the very Bank of Heaven and claim its fulfillment by all the power of His omnipotence and the sanctions of His faithfulness. Why, the very added clause itself, "as it is in heaven," implies that the fulfillment of this petition would change earth into a heaven and bring heaven into every one of our lives in the measure which we meet this lofty prayer! This petition, therefore, while it implies the spirit of absolute submission, rises to the height of illimitable faith.

Beloved, have we understood it and learned thus to pray, "Thy will be done in earth, as it is in heaven"?

It teaches us that prayer may include all our natural and temporal wants and should be accompanied by the spirit of trustful dependence upon our Father's care for the supply of all our earthly needs. "Give us this day our daily bread" gives to every child of God the right to claim a Father's supporting and providing love. It is wonderful how much spiritual blessing we get by praying and trusting for temporal needs. They greatly curtail the fullness of their spiritual life and separate God's personal providence from the most simple and minute of life's secular interests who try, through second causes or through ample human provision, to be independent of His direct interposition and care. We are to recognize every means of support and temporal link of blessing as directly from His hand, and to commit every interest of business and life to His direction and blessing.

At the same time, it is implied that there must be in this a spirit of simplicity and daily trust. It is not the bread of future days we ask, but the bread of today. Nor is it always luxurious bread, the bread of affluence, the banquet, and the feast, but daily bread, or rather as the best authorities translate it, "sufficient bread," bread such as He sees to be really best for us. It may not be always bread and butter; it may be homely bread, and it may be sometimes scant bread, but He can make even that sufficient and add such a blessing with it and such an impartation of His life and strength as will make us know, like our Master in the wilderness, that "Man shall not live by bread alone, but by every word that proceedeth out of the mouth of God." It implies, in short, a spirit of contentment and satisfaction with our daily lot and a trust that leaves tomorrow's needs in His wise and faithful hand to care for us day by day as each new morrow comes.

Beloved, have you thus learned to pray for temporal things, bringing all your life to God? Bringing it in the spirit of daily trust and thankful contentment with your simple lot and your Father's wisdom and faithfulness?

It teaches us that true prayer must ever recognize our need of the mercy of God. There are two versions of this petition, "Forgive us our trespasses" and "Forgive us our debts." This is not accidental. There may be an honest consciousness in the heart of the suppliant that there has been no willful or known disobedience or sin, and yet there may be infinite debt, omission, and shortcoming as compared with the high standard of God's holiness and even our own ideal. The sensitive and thoroughly quickened spirit will never reach a place where it will not be sensible of so much more to which it is reaching out and God is pressing it forward, that it will not need to say, "Forgive us our debts," even where perhaps it could not conscientiously say, "Forgive us our transgressions."

This sense of demerit on our part throws us constantly upon the merits and righteousness of our Great High Priest and makes our prayers forever more dependent on His intercession and offered in His name. This enables the most unworthy to "come boldly unto the throne of grace" to "obtain mercy, and find grace to help in time of need." We do not mean that our dear Lord encourages us to expect to be constantly sinning and repenting, for the final petition of this prayer is for complete deliverance from all evil, but He graciously stoops to the lowest level and yet grades the prayer so as to cover the experience of the highest saint, to meet the finer sense of the most sanctified spirit as well as the coarser consciousness of actual sin on the part of the humblest penitent.

This petition presupposes a very solemn spirit of forgiveness in the heart of the suppliant. This is indispensable to the acceptance of the prayer for forgiveness. The Greek construction, and the use of the aorist tense, expresses a very practical shade of meaning, namely, that the forgiveness of the injury that has been done to us has preceded our prayer for divine forgiveness. Freely translated, it should be thus expressed, "Forgive us our trespasses, as we have already forgiven them that trespassed against us."

There are certain spiritual states, therefore, that are indispensable to acceptable prayer, even for the simplest mercies, and without which we cannot pray. The soul that is filled with bitterness cannot approach God in communion. Inferentially, it must therefore be true that the soul that is cherishing any other sin and sinful state is thereby hindered from access to the throne of grace. This is an Old Testament truth that all the abundant grace of the New Testament has not provoked nor weakened. "If I regard iniquity in my heart, the Lord will not hear me" was a lesson which even David learned in his sad and solemn experience. "I will wash mine hands in innocency: so will I compass thine altar" is the eternal condition of acceptable communion with the Holy One. The most sinful may come for mercy, but they must put away their sin and freely forgive the sins of others. Above all others, there seem to be two unpardonable sins: one, the sin which willfully rejects the Holy Spirit and the Savior presented by Him, that is, the sin of willful unbelief; and the other, the sin of unforgivingness.

It teaches us that prayer is our true weapon and safeguard in the temptations of life, and that we may rightly claim the divine protection from our spiritual adversaries. This petition, "Lead us not into temptation," undoubtedly covers the whole field of our spiritual conflicts and may be interpreted, in the largest sense, of all we need to arm us against our spiritual enemies. It cannot strictly mean that we pray to be kept from all

temptation, for God Himself has said, "Blessed is the man
that endureth temptation," and "Count it all joy when ye
fall into diverse temptation," and, "Let patience have her
perfect work." It rather means, "Lead us not into a crisis
of temptation," "and lead us so that we shall not fall under
temptation or be tried above what we are able to bear."
There are spiritual trials and crises which come to souls,
too hard for them to bear, snares into which multitudes
fall; and this is the peculiar promise which this prayer
claims, that they shall not come into any such crisis, but
shall be kept out of situations which would be too trying,
carried through the places which would be too narrow,
and kept safe from peril.

This is what is meant by the word "The Lord knoweth
how to deliver the godly out of temptations," and also the
still more gracious promise in First Corinthians 10:13:
"There hath no temptation taken you but such as is
common to man: but God is faithful, who will not suffer
you to be tempted above that ye are able; but will with
the temptation also make a way to escape, that ye may be
able to bear it." When we think how many there are who
perish in the snare, and how narrow the path often is, oh,
what comfort it should give us to know that our Lord has
authorized us to claim His divine protection in these awful
perils to meet the wiles of the devil and the insidious foes
against whom all our skill would be unavailing!

This was the Master's own solemn admonition to His
disciples in the garden in the hour and power of darkness,

"Watch and pray, that ye enter not into temptation." And this was His own safeguard in that hour. The apostle has given it to us as the unceasing prescription of wisdom and safety in connection with our spiritual conflict, "Praying always with all prayer and supplication in the Spirit, and watching thereunto with all perseverance and supplication for all saints." "Continue in prayer, and watch in the same with thanksgiving."

The crowning petition of the Lord's Prayer is a petition for entire sanctification, including deliverance from every other form of evil. "Deliver us from evil." This has frequently been translated "from the evil one," but the neuter gender contradicts this and renders it most natural to translate it, as the old version does, of evil in all forms rather than the author of evil. This is more satisfactory to the Christian heart. There are many forms of evil which do not come from the evil one. We have as much cause to pray against ourselves as against the devil. And there are physical evils covered by this petition as well as special temptations. It is a petition, therefore, against sin, sickness, and sorrow in every form in which they could be evils. It is a prayer for our complete deliverance from all the effects of the Fall, in spirit, soul and body. It is a prayer which echoes the fourfold gospel and the fullness of Jesus in the highest and widest measure. It teaches us that we may expect victory over the power of sin, support against the attacks of sickness, triumph over all sorrow and a life in which all things shall be only good and work together for good according to God's high purpose. Surely the prayer of the Holy Spirit for such a blessing is the best pledge of the answer! Let us not be afraid to claim it in all its fullness.

All prayer should end with praise and believing confidence. The Lord's Prayer, according to the most correct manuscripts, really ends with "Deliver us from evil," but later copies contain the closing clause, "For thine is the kingdom, and the power, and the glory for ever. Amen." And while it is extremely doubtful whether our Lord uttered these words, yet they have so grown into the phraseology of Christendom that we may, without danger, draw from them our closing lessons.

The doxology expresses the spirit of praise and consecration. We ascribe to God the authority and power to do what we have asked, and give the glory of it to His name; and then, in token of our confidence that He will do so, we add the Amen, which simply means "So let it be done." In fact, it is faith ascending to the throne and humbly claiming and commanding in the name of Jesus that for which humility has petitioned. Our Lord does require this element of faith and this acknowledgment and attestation of His faithfulness as a condition of answered prayer. No prayer is complete therefore until faith has added its "Amen."

Such, then, are some of the principle teachings of this universal prayer. How often our lips have uttered it! Beloved, has it searched our hearts this day and shown us the imperfection, the selfishness, the smallness, the unbelief of what we call prayer? Let us henceforth repeat its pregnant words with deeper thoughtfulness and weigh them with more solemn realization than we have done before, until they shall come to be to us what they indeed are, the summary of all prayer, the expression of all possible need and blessing and the language of a worship like that of the holy ranks who continually surround the throne above. Then indeed shall His kingdom come and His will be done on earth as it is in heaven.

Beautiful and blessed prayer! How it recalls the most sacred associations of life! How it follows the prodigal even in his deepest downfall and his latest moments! How it expands with the deepening spiritual life of the saint! How it wafts the latest aspirations and adorations of the departing Christian to the throne to which he is ready to wing his way! Let it be more dear to us henceforth, more real, more deep, wider and higher, as it teaches us to pray and wings our petition to the throne of grace. And, oh, if there be anyone reading these words now who has often uttered it without having any right to say "Our Father," or any real ability to enter into its heart-searching meaning, may you this very moment, beloved reader, stop; and as you think with tears of the lips that once taught you its tender accents years ago, but that are silent now in the molding grave, kneel down at the feet of that mother's God, that father's God, that sister's God; and if you are willing to say, "Forgive us our trespasses as we forgive those that trespass against us," you may dare to add, linked in everlasting hope and fellowship with those that first voiced those words to you, "Our Father, which art in heaven."

On a lonely bed in a Southern hospital, a soldier lay dying. A Christian friend called to see him and tried to speak of Christ, but was repelled with infidel scorn. Once or twice he tried in vain to reach his heart, but at last simply knelt down by the bed and tenderly repeated the Lord's Prayer, slowly and solemnly. When he arose to leave, the infidel's eyes were wet with tears. He tried to brush them away and conceal his feelings, but at last broke down and said, "My mother taught me that more than fifty years ago, and it quite broke me up to hear it again." The missionary passed away, not wishing to hinder the voice of God. The next time he called, the patient had disappeared. Sending for the nurse he asked about him and was told that a night or two before the soldier had died, but just before the end she heard him repeating the words, "Our Father, who art in heaven," and then he seemed to add in a husky voice: "Mother, I am coming! He is my Father, too."

Dear friend, let this old prayer become to you a holy bond with all that is dearest on earth and a stepping-stone to the very gates of heaven!

~ 2 ~

Encouragements to Prayer

"And he said unto them, Which of you
shall have a friend, and shall go unto him
at midnight, and say unto him, Friend,
lend me three loaves; for a friend of mine
in his journey is come to me, and I have
nothing to set before him? And he from
within shall answer and say, Trouble me
not: the door is now shut, and my children
are with me in bed; I cannot rise and give
thee. I say unto you, Though he will not
rise and give him, because he is his friend,
yet because of his importunity he will rise
and give him as many as he needeth. And
I say unto you, Ask, and it shall be given
you; seek, and ye shall find; knock, and it
shall be opened unto you. For every one

that asketh receiveth; and he that seeketh findeth; and to him that knocketh it shall be opened. If a son shall ask bread of any of you that is a father, will he give him a stone? Or if he asks a fish, will he for a fish give him a serpent? Or if he shall ask an egg, will he offer him a scorpion? If ye then, being evil, know how to give good gifts unto your children: how much more shall your heavenly Father give the Holy Spirit to them that ask him?" (Luke 11:5–13).

THIS IS OUR SAVIOR's second teaching about prayer. His first was an actual example of prayer. This is an unfolding of some of the special encouragements to prayer which are afforded by the gracious care of God, our Father and Friend, and also some deeper instructions respecting the nature and spirit of true prayer.

God is our Father. This had already been suggested in the opening words of the Lord's Prayer, but it is amplified in this passage by a comparison between the earthly and heavenly Parent: "If ye then, being evil, know how to give good gifts unto your children: how much more shall your heavenly Father give the Holy Spirit to them that ask him?" God is not only a Father, but much more than any earthly father. How much this expresses to many of us! There are few who cannot recall, in the memories of home, the value of a father's or a mother's love and care; or, if they have been wanting, all the more, perhaps, has the orphaned heart felt its deep need and reached out for a father's heart and hand. Who of us has not felt in some great emergency, needing a wisdom and resource beyond our own, "Oh, if my father were only here," or, perhaps, has said to God: "If Thou wert my earthly father now, Thou wouldst sit down by my side and let me tell Thee of all my perplexity, and Thou wouldst tell me just what to do, and then wouldst do for me what I cannot do for myself." And yet His presence is as real as if we saw Him, and we may as freely pour our hearts out with all their fears and griefs and know that He hears and helps as no earthly father is able to do either in love or relief. Perhaps even better than the memory of our childhood is the realization of our own fatherhood or motherhood. Who that has ever felt a parent's love can fail to understand this appeal? It is a love which neither the helplessness nor the worthlessness of its object can affect. It is a love which often has gladly sacrificed everything, even life itself, for the loved one. But it was from the bosom of God that all that love came at first, and infinitely more is still in reserve. The depth and length and height of this "much more" can only be measured by the distance between the infinite and the human. Much more than you love your child does He love you; much more than you would give or sacrifice is He ready to bestow and has He already sacrificed; much more than you can trust or ask a father for, may you dare to bring to Him; much more unerring is His wisdom, illimitable His power, and inexhaustible His love! Shall we, then, with the little alphabet of our human experience, try to spell out all His love and learn the deeper meaning of the prayer, "Our Father, which art in heaven"?

He is our Friend. "Which of you shall have a friend?" This also finds its full significance through the actual experience of each one of us. Who has not had a friend, and more of a friend in some respects than even a father? There are intimacies not born of human blood that are the most intense and lasting bonds of earthly love. Jonathan was more to David than Jesse was, and Timothy was more to Paul than a very son. How much our friends have been to us! One by one, let us count them over, recall each act and bond of love, and think of all that we may trust them for and all in which they stood by us; and then, as we concentrate the whole weight of recollection and affection, let us put God in that place of confidence and think He is all that and infinitely more. Our Friend! The One who is personally interested in us; Who has set His heart upon us; Who has made Himself acquainted with us; Who has come near to us in the tender and delicate intimacy of unspeakable fellowship; Who has spoken to us such gracious words; Who has given us such invaluable pledges and promises; Who has done so much for us; Who has made such priceless sacrifices, and Who, we feel, is ready to take any trouble or go to any expense to aid us to Him we are coming in prayer, our Heavenly Friend.

He is a Friend in extremity. The case here supposed is a hard one. The supplicant is in great need, has a case of suffering on his hands, and is wholly without means to meet it. It may represent any emergency in our lives. Other friends are for fair weather. This is always God's time.

> The friends who in our sunshine live,
>> When winter comes, have flown,
> And he who has but tears to give
>> Must weep those tears alone.

But this Friend has authorized us to claim His help especially in times of need. "Call upon me," He says, "in the day of trouble; I will deliver thee, and thou shalt glorify me." "God is our refuge and strength, a very present help in time of trouble." "Thou hast known my soul in adversities" is the testimony of one who proved His faithful friendship under the severest pressure. "God that comforteth those that are cast down," "The Father of mercies, and the God of all comfort" are His chosen names and titles. Let us not fear, therefore, to come to Him when we have nothing to bring to Him but our grief and fear. We shall be welcome. He is able for the hardest occasions, and He is seated on His throne for the very purpose of giving help in time of need. Even if the case seems wholly helpless, and the hour is as dark as the dark midnight of this parable, cast thy burden on the Lord— yes, all your care, for "he careth for you," and "the Lord is nigh unto them that are of a broken heart; and saveth such as be of a contrite spirit."

He is a Friend, not only in season, but at all seasons, and at the most unseasonable times. This parable is the story of a man coming to his friend when all reasonable ground for expecting a favorable reception was out of the question It was midnight. The door was shut, literally barred, the house closed for the night, and the time for calls long past. Nevertheless that door was opened, that petition heard, that favor granted, and whatever may be the meaning of the reluctance of the earthly friend, certainly we know that the heavenly Friend assures us that none of these causes will prevent His hearing and helping in the most extreme and desperate straits and seasons. The peculiarity of God's grace is that He helps when man would refuse to help, and its highest trophies are associated with hours when mercy seemed long past and hope forever dead.

Look at that wicked king, Manasseh, who for half a century was a brutal butcher of the prophets and saints of God. He had literally fed his brutality on the wreck of all that was sacred and divine. And then the hand of retribution struck him down and left him in his miserable old age a captive in a foreign prison. One would have thought that prayer from such a man was profanity, and that all heaven would shut its ears at the very idea of his escaping condign and merciless punishment. But in that late hour Manasseh cried to the Lord in his affliction, and the Lord heard him and had mercy on him, forgave him all his sins, and brought him again into his kingdom. And then Manasseh knew that the Lord was God. Surely no soul can ever say again that the hour is too late or the door too strongly barred for mercy!

Look at that city Nineveh, the oppressor of the nations, the proud queen of Assyria, the scourge of Israel and Judah, the boastful shrine of every abominable idolatry! At length its iniquities reached to heaven, and the prophet Jonah was sent to proclaim its speedy and certain doom. "Yet forty days, and Nineveh shall be overthrown." That city went upon its knees; its kings, its priests, its princes, and its peasantry were prostrated in penitential prayer, and the barred gates were opened, the doors of mercy were unlocked, the terrible decree was revoked, and Nineveh became a monument of the mercy of God; the very children in its streets and the cattle in its stalls being specified as the objects of His tender compassion!

Look at King Hezekiah to whom, in the fullness of his prosperity, the message came, "Set thine house in order; for thou shalt die, and not live." Surely that looked like a closing and barring of the gates of the tomb. The sentence fell on his ears like a voice of doom. But in that hour Hezekiah prayed. A poor and trembling prayer it was: "I reckoned till morning, that, as a lion, so will he break all my bones: from day even to night wilt thou make an end of me. Like a crane or a swallow, so did I chatter: I did mourn as a dove: mine eyes fail with looking upward." Though there was little faith in that heartbroken gasp of prayer, it reached the heart of God, and the decree that had seemed imperative and inexorable, the stern word that had set a barrier like adamant to the path of life and opened the cold stone portals of what seemed an inevitable tomb, was changed, and the messenger was sent back with the gracious reprieve, "I will add unto thy days fifteen years."

Such is the Friend to whom we pray, Who stands between us and all the mighty bars and doors of material force, of natural law, of human purpose, and even of divine judgment, and turns aside with His hands of love every bolt and bar which stands between us and the fullest blessing which He can give our trusting and obedient hearts. Shall we ever again think anything too hard, or any hour too late? He loves the hour of extremity. It is His chosen time of Almighty interposition. "God will help her at the turning of the morning" is His voice to Zion.

Summoned to the dying couch of a little girl, the mighty Master had time to tarry by the way until a poor, helpless woman was healed by the touch of His garment. But meanwhile that little life had ebbed away, and human unbelief hastened to turn back the visit which was now too late. "Thy daughter is dead; trouble not the Master." It was then that His strong and mighty love rose to its glorious height of power and victory. "Fear not," was His calm reply; "believe only, and she shall be made whole."

Yes, let us go at midnight, for He that keeps Israel neither slumbers nor sleeps. Let us go when all other doors are barred and even the heavens seem brass, for the gates of prayer are open evermore, and it is only when the sun is gone down and our pillow is but the stone of the wilderness that we behold the ladder that reaches unto heaven, with our infinite God above it and the angels of His providence ascending and descending for our help and deliverance. "Men ought always to pray, and not to faint."

He is a Friend that will not deceive us. He will not give us a stone for bread; that is, a barren, worthless, empty answer, but a real and satisfying blessing. He will not give us a serpent when we come for a fish; that is, a harmful gift, or one that contains a hidden snare of temptation or spiritual evil. Many of the things that we ask in our blindness have serpents coiled in their folds, but He loves us too well to give us such an answer, and sometimes, therefore, He must modify or refuse our petition if He would be our true Father in heaven. And we need not fear to trust this to Him or make the boldest requests lest they might do us harm, for He who gives the greatest blessing can give the grace to keep it from being a selfish idol or a spiritual curse. People sometimes say, "If God were to heal me or give me some temporal blessing for which I am praying, I fear it might not be best for me." Can we not trust Him for the grace as well as the gift?

And again, our Father will not give us a scorpion if we ask an egg; that is, something that would leave a bitterness and a sting behind. "The blessing of the Lord, it maketh rich, and he addeth no sorrow with it." How many earthly roses fade and leave a lasting thorn! How many drops from earthly cups have more dregs of poison than drops of joy! How many a love and friendship but adds to the sorrow of the parting and to the bitterness of the memory. But all that heaven gives us are everlasting joys. Let us trust Him for all we ask, and we shall have eternal cause to sing of His love and faithfulness.

This Friend gives full measure. "He will rise and give him as many as he needeth." In our Father's house there is bread enough and to spare. His measure is more abundantly. Three loaves He gave to the hungry wayfarer. Nay, three were asked; He seems to have given far more, at least, was willing to give as many as were needed. These three may be suggestive of our threefold life and God's complete provision for it in every part—spirit, soul and body. Have we claimed the ample measure? Are we satisfied today and running over with superabundant life and love for the hungry wayfarers that come to us? He only asked it as a loan, but he received it as a gift, the only return required being thanks and love. So our Father and our Friend is ready to supply all our need "according to his riches in glory by Christ Jesus." Let us come, exclaiming,

My soul, ask what thou wilt,
　Thou canst not be too bold.
Since His own blood for thee He spilt,
　What else can He withhold?
Beyond thy utmost wants,
　His power and love can bless;
To trusting souls He loves to grant
　More than they can express.

In its simplest form, prayer is represented as asking. "Ask, and it shall be given unto you." This expresses the most elementary form of prayer—the presenting of our petitions to God in the simplest terms and manner, and we are undoubtedly taught that even the most ordinary and imperfect request which is sincerely presented at the throne of grace receives the attention and response of our heavenly Father. It is probable that no honest heart ever asks in vain, even where, through ignorance or inexperience, it may but partly understand the principles and conditions of effectual prayer. The infant's helpless cry reaches the mother's heart not more surely than the feeblest gasp of need and supplication from His children's lips.

There is a higher form of prayer, "Seek, and ye shall find." This denotes the prayer that waits upon God until it receives an answer, and that follows up that answer in obedience to His direction until it finds all it seeks, whether of light, or health, or strength from on high.

This is the prayer that inquires of the Lord, hearkens to catch His answer, and hastens to obey it—"watching at his gates; waiting daily at the posts of his doors"; "following on to know the Lord," and finding, as it follows, full light, help, and blessing. For prayer is more than asking; it is a receiving, a waiting, a learning of Him, a converse and communion, in which He has much to say and we have much to learn. This is the prayer that has brought us so often His peace, His heavenly baptism of love and power, His blessed working out of the problems of our life; and it is of this He says in such oft-repeated promises, "Let none that wait on thee be ashamed." "I said not unto the seed of Jacob, Seek ye me in vain." "They that seek the Lord shall not lack any good thing." For prayer is not an asking for things so much as a seeking for Himself and a pressing into that fellowship which is beyond all other gifts and which carries with it every needed blessing.

There is a knocking prayer, to which the promise is given, "Knock, and it shall be opened unto you." This is more than seeking. This is the prayer that surmounts the great obstacles of life, the closed doors of circumstances, the brazen gates and adamantine mountains of hindrance and opposition, and which, in the name of our ascended Lord and in the fellowship of His mediatorial rights and powers, presses through every obstacle and treads down every adversary. It is not so much the prayer that knocks at the gates of heaven and extorts an answer from an unwilling God as the prayer which, having received the

40

answer and promise, carries it forth against the gates of the enemy and beats them down, as the walls of Jericho fell before the tramp and shout of Israel's believing hosts. It is the prayer which takes its place at the side of our ascended Lord and claims what He has promised to give, and even commands, in His mighty name, that which He has already commanded through His royal Priesthood and all-prevailing intercession. It is faith putting its hand on the omnipotence of God and using it in fellowship with our Omnipotent Head until it sees His name prevail against all that opposes His will, the crooked things made straight, the gates of brass opened, and the fetters of iron broken asunder.

It is Moses standing on the Mount with God while Joshua fights in the plain below, holding up the hands of victorious faith, seeing the hosts of Joshua keep step with his uplifted hands and the battle advance or ebb as those hands went up or down, until they waved on high over a victorious field and proclaimed the memorial name, "Jehovah-Nissi, the Lord is my banner," a name which has become our watchword from generation to generation. It is written, "Because the Lord hath sworn that the Lord will have war with Amalek from generation to generation." It is when our hand is upon the throne of the Lord that He wages war with all our enemies, and they fall before His victorious will.

It is Deborah, kneeling in her tent that day when Barak led the host of Israel against the legions of Sisera, feeling in her great heart the surging tides of that glorious warfare, and knowing by the throbs of her faith and prayer when the battle waxed or waned, until she had fought it all over upon the field of vision; and as she claimed the last victorious onset and commanded the last foe to flee in Jehovah's name, her exulting spirit shouted in the victory of faith, though perhaps her eyes had not seen the battlefield at all, "O my soul, thou hast trodden down strength." Her soul had trodden down the foe; her spirit had triumphed in the conscious power of Jehovah; her faith had knocked at the gates of the enemy until the wall of adamant was laid in the dust and the gates of brass were shivered into fragments and scattered as by the whirlwinds of the sky. This is "the effectual prayer" which "availeth much."

We are also instructed to come in the spirit of boldness and importunity. "Because of his importunity he will rise and give him as many as he needeth." This is a very difficult passage and one that has been variously interpreted. Dr. Walker, the thoughtful author of *The Philosophy of the Plan of Salvation*, has endeavored to show in his work on the Holy Spirit that this word here means "extremity," and that the idea conveyed is not that the man is heard because of his continued prayer, but because of his extreme distress and the difficult emergency which is facing him. We cannot find, however, sufficient authority for this view. The Greek word literally means "without shamefacedness." It is the negative form of the word "shamefacedness," which occurs in First Timothy 2:9, and it properly means boldness and audacity. There is nothing whatever unscriptural in this truth, which, indeed, is constantly reiterated in the New Testament, that we are to come boldly to the throne of grace, and, without timidity, for Jesus' sake, claim our redemption rights in all their fullness. "We have boldness and access," we are told, "by the faith of Him." "Having therefore . . . boldness to enter into the holiest by the blood of Jesus . . . let us draw near with a true heart in full assurance of faith." "Let us therefore come boldly unto the throne of grace."

There is no doubt that if Esther had hesitated to enter into the presence of the king at the crisis of her country's fate, she would have both lost her blessing and risked the fortunes of her nation. There is no doubt that if modest Ruth had feared to claim her lawful rights at the feet of Boaz under the law of the kinsman, she probably would never have been his bride nor the mother of the long and honored line of kings, commencing with David and ending with the Son of Man. And there is no doubt that our unbelieving fear and shrinking timorousness have lost us many a redemption right, and that a bold and victorious confidence which claims its inheritance in the name of our risen and ascended Lord is pleasing to God. And we believe this is the meaning and teaching of this beautiful parable—that we are to come boldly to our Father and our Friend, no matter what doors would seem to be closed or what discouragements may frown across our way. Someone has said that the secret of success in human affairs has often been audacity. There is, at least, a holy audacity in Christian life and faith which is not inconsistent with the profoundest humility, and in which lies the secret of the victorious achievements of a Moses, a Joshua, an Elijah, and a Daniel in the Old Testament, and of the Syro-Phoenician woman and the glorious apostle of faith in the New, as well as the Luther's and the Careys who have been pioneers of gospel truth and missionary triumph in the Christian dispensation.

Perhaps the highest ministry of prayer is prayer for others. This petition was not for the suppliant himself but for a friend of his, who, in his journey, had come to him and found the larder empty and nothing to set before him. Literally it means a friend "who had lost his way."

How tenderly it suggests the need of those for whom we have constantly to come to our heavenly Friend. It is of this that the Apostle James says in referring to prayer, "Confess your faults one to another, and pray one for another, that ye may be healed. The effectual fervent prayer of a righteous man availeth much." And then with special reference to this very case he adds, "Brethren, if any of you do err from the truth, and one convert him; let him know, that he which converteth the sinner from the error of his way shall . . . hide a multitude of sins." Thank God that we can bring to Him these cases that have lost their way—our unsaved friends, our wandering sons and daughters, our brethren who have gone back from their first love and the blessedness they knew when first they saw the Lord—and He will not refuse to hear their cry nor fail to give them the living Bread.

Often our boldest prayer will be the prayer for others. For ourselves we may fear perhaps a selfish motive, but for them we know it is the prayer of love; and if it be the prayer that seeks His glory, we can claim for it His mighty and prevailing will and intercession. Oh, you who have often felt your way closed for service, this is a ministry that all can exercise, and is the mightiest ministry of life! Let us be encouraged henceforth to use it in fellowship with Him who has spent the centuries that have passed since His ascension in praying for others and representing us as our great High Priest before the throne.

The last lesson that this passage teaches us about prayer is that the Holy Spirit is the source and substance of all that prayer can ask, and a gift that carries with it the pledge of all other gifts and blessings.

"How much more shall your heavenly Father give the Holy Spirit to them that ask Him?" This is spoken as if there were really nothing else to ask. It is still more remarkable that in the parallel passage in Matthew, the language used is, "How much more shall your Father which is in heaven give good things to them that ask him?" So then "the Holy Spirit" and "good things" are synonymous. He that has the Holy Spirit shall have all good things. Was not that the symbolical meaning of the widow's oil in the ancient miracle? Her pot of oil, poured out into all the empty vessels, became sufficient to pay all her debts and furnish an income for all her future life. All she needed was the pot of oil; it was currency for every blessing. So is the Holy Spirit. He that has this heavenly gift is in touch with the throne of infinite grace and the God of infinite fullness, and there is nothing that he cannot claim. Oh, when shall we learn to seek first the kingdom of God and His righteousness, and know that all these things shall be added unto us!

Dean Alford calls attention to a beautiful Greek construction in this closing verse in the reference to our heavenly Father. The verse "your heavenly Father" in the original is, literally, "your Father out of heaven." In the Lord's Prayer a few verses previously it is "Our Father which art in heaven," but here the preposition is changed and it is "your Father *out of* heaven." Why is this blessed and stupendous change? Our Father has already begun to move toward us and to enter our hearts by the Holy Spirit whom He has just sent to make a heaven below for every praying heart. So while we begin our prayer with our eyes directed upward, we end it with our inmost being filled with the presence and fullness of God and the throne of His abiding grace and power.

Blessed and heavenly altar of incense, standing by the rent veil, and breathing forth its incense into the outer and inner chambers, oh, let us be found forever there!

> Where heaven comes down our souls to greet;
> And glory crowns the Mercy Seat.

~ 3 ~

In His Name

"And in that day ye shall ask me nothing. Verily, verily, I say unto you, Whatsoever ye shall ask the Father in my name, he will give it you. Hitherto have ye asked nothing in my name: ask, and ye shall receive, that your joy may be full. These things have I spoken unto you in proverbs: but the time cometh, when I shall no more speak unto you in proverbs, but I shall show you plainly of the Father. At that day ye shall ask in my name: and I say not unto you, that I will pray the Father for you: for the Father himself loveth you, because ye have loved me, and have believed that I came out from God" (John 16:23–27).

A. B. Simpson

"FOR JESUS' SAKE," "in Jesus' name" are phrases familiar to every ear and tongue in Christendom, but how little they are thoroughly understood we shall probably find as we glance at their deeper meaning. This is the profound teaching about prayer which the Master chiefly emphasizes in His closing addresses to His disciples.

Undoubtedly it means this much at least: that we are to pray to the Father as revealed in Jesus Christ.

"Whatsoever ye shall ask the Father in my name" might be translated "Whatsoever ye shall ask the Father as represented by me." It expresses Christ's identity with the Father. The Father had been known to them before by many different names: "Elohim," the God of nature; "El Shaddai," the God of power; "Adonai," the God of providence; "Jehovah," the God of covenant grace; but henceforth, He is to be known as "Jehovah-Jesus," God in Christ. This is undoubtedly implied in the language of this passage and involved in the thought to which the Savior is giving expression. It is the same thought that He repeats in the parallel verse, "Whatsoever ye shall ask in my name, that will I do, that the Father may be glorified in the Son." There it plainly expresses that the Father and Son are acting in perfect concert, and it is through the Son only that the Father is glorified and revealed to man or understood by him.

The idea may be carried so far as to do away with the distinct personality of the Father and the Son, and this,

48

of course, would be extreme and erroneous. But bearing this in mind and recognizing fully the dual personality, it is true that the Father Himself is revealed to us in the person of the Son, and that we are to ask the Father for our petitions and feel encouraged to expect His gracious answer because of what we know of Jesus, through Whose presence and teachings He Himself has become revealed to us. Would we come with confidence to our Savior? Let us come with the same confidence to His Father, for "He that hath seen me hath seen the Father." The words that He has spoken, the Father that dwelt in Him spoke. The love that He manifested was the Father's love, Whom He came to reveal. He is the brightness of that Father's glory, the express image of His person, and the reflection of His will and character. It is to God in Christ, therefore, that we are to pray; to the God and Father of our Lord Jesus Christ; to Him, of Whom we know nothing except through the Son, and in Whom we trust, even as in Jesus Himself. Thus let us learn to pray in the Name of Jesus.

This expression, however, denotes far more than the identity of the Father and the Son. It expresses the great truth of mediation and intercession.

Not only do we come to the Father as we know Him in Jesus, but we come to Him *through* the Mediator. There are deep necessities for this in the nature of God and the relationships of sinful men with Him. So deeply did Job realize this that he cried out for a Daysman who could "lay his hand upon us both," some being that could touch at once both heaven and earth and bring them into harmony and fellowship. This is just what Christ has done. His incarnation has bridged over the infinite gulf between the eternal and spiritual Deity and finite man, and His atonement has healed the awful breach that had morally and imperatively separated the sinner from a holy God. Like the dying mother who, with her latest breath, reached out one hand to her husband and the other to her boy and, drawing both hands together, united them upon her dying breast and covered them with her tears and benedictions; so Jesus in His death has united the sinner with his offended God, praying, "Father, forgive them; for they know not what they do," and appealing to sinful men, "Be ye reconciled to God."

But not only has He brought God and men into reconciliation and fellowship, but He keeps that fellowship unbroken by His ceaseless intercession. "He ever liveth to make intercession for [us]," and, therefore, "is able also to save them to the uttermost that come unto God by him."

This idea of mediation is widely illustrated in the Holy Scriptures. We see it in the story of Joseph and his relation to Pharaoh and the Egyptians. "Go to Joseph," was the king's response to all who came to him for relief or judgment. All the affairs of the kingdom were entrusted to his administration, and he was the mediator and channel of all communication. We see it in the beautiful story of Esther as she ventured to touch the golden scepter and stand between her people and their oppressor and danger; and by her courage and patriotism she saved her nation from extinction. Still more impressively was it foreshadowed in the ministry of Moses, who became, at Sinai, the channel of communication between God and the terrified people. "Speak thou with us," was their cry, "but let not God speak with us lest we die"; and God consented to use Moses as the channel of His revelations to Israel and to teach the lesson of our Great Mediator.

But the most striking of all the ancient types of Christ our Mediator was Aaron, the Hebrew high priest. It was his special office to stand between the people and God and present their worship in the Holy of Holies and make intercession for their sins and needs. For them he passed through the open veil, stood beneath the Shekinah, presented the blood and incense at the mercy seat, and came back to them with the benediction of Jehovah. In all this he was but the type of the better ministry of the Great High Priest in the true Tabernacle of heaven. There He has entered, with His own blood, through the rent veil of His own flesh, now to appear in the presence of God for us.

The ministry of Aaron may well express the deeper meaning of His High Priesthood. Upon his heart the ancient priest continually carried, engraven in precious jewels, the names of Israel's tribes, and this was but to teach us that Christ, our Great High Priest, perpetually carries upon His heart our names, engraven in imperishable characters and worn as jewels of ornament and pride,

51

even amid the glories of the heavenly world. It does not merely mean that He prays for us occasionally or takes our petitions and presents them to His Father. That, undoubtedly, He does, but He prays for us ten thousand times when we are too ignorant or too forgetful to pray for ourselves, and every moment He holds our names before His Father in unforgetting love and ceaseless remembrance. And not only upon his heart, but the ancient priest carried them also upon his shoulders. So, upon the strong arms of His omnipotence, our ascended Lord continually bears our burdens, as strong to help as He is swift to hear.

The ancient priest bore upon his brow a beautiful and significant symbol, a coronet with jeweled letters carrying the significant words, "Holiness to the Lord." This he was continually to bear as often as he entered the Holy Place, that he might bear the iniquities of the children of Israel in their holy things. So, our blessed Intercessor bears upon His brow this inscription, not for Himself, for His holiness is never questioned, but as the proclamation of our holiness and perfect acceptance. He covers the imperfection of our holiest services with His perfect righteousness and keeps us constantly accepted in the presence of holy angels and the infinite and heart-searching God. What infinite meaning these figures give to the simple words, "In his name!" How wide they open the gates of prayer, and how perfect the consolation they give to the timid heart! "Seeing, then, that we have a great high priest, that is passed into the heavens, Jesus the Son of God . . . let us therefore come boldly unto the throne of grace, that we may obtain mercy, and find grace to help in time of need."

"In his name" signifies that our prayers are to be grounded upon the finished work of Christ and our redemption rights through His death and atonement.

Indeed, His very intercession for us is based upon His sufferings and blood. It is on the ground of the cross and the accomplished redemption that He claims for us all the purchase of His blood and all the promises of the everlasting covenant.

We are all familiar with the incident of the brave soldier who had often pleaded for the pardon of his unworthy brother and saved his life from public execution on account of desertion, but at last had been told by his kind general that it was useless to plead any more, because if he repeated the offense, it would be absolutely necessary in the interests of public order that the penalty should be required. Unfortunately, the reckless man soon repeated the offense, and the sentence of the court-martial was about to be pronounced without mercy. Then the general, noticing the brave old soldier weeping silently in the ranks, asked him if he had anything to say for his brother, but the old veteran simply stood up and raising aloft the stump of his amputated arm, he silently held it up, while the great tears rolled down his cheeks, and many wept around him as they thought of all it meant of sacrifice and devotion to his country. That was all his plea. He knew that words were useless now, but he held up the pledge of his sufferings and love, and let it plead more eloquently than speech for his brother's forfeited life. And eloquently it did plead, for, with tears of emotion, the old commander answered, "Sit down, my brave fellow, you shall have your brother's life. He is unworthy of it, but you have purchased it by your blood."

It is thus our ascended Redeemer pleads for us. He does not beg for mercy that would be simply gratuitous and unbought, but He boldly asks for that which is His purchased right, and for which His own blood has been sacrificed. Long before the incarnation and the cross, He had entered into a covenant with the Father; and God had promised, by His immutable oath, that if He would bear the sins of men and settle for all the penalties of a holy law, He should receive as His mediatorial right forgiveness for every penitent and believing sinner who should accept His gospel, and all the resources of grace that should be needed to consummate the salvation of every sinner. And now He simply claims His redemption rights and our rights through Him by virtue of that promise.

Asking in Jesus' name, therefore, is asking that for which Jesus has suffered and died, and which He has freely, fully purchased for all His own. Surely with such a plea, we may come boldly to the throne of grace and ask as much as the precious blood of Calvary is worthy to claim, and how much that is, it will take all eternity to tell. This is the strong ground of our prayer for salvation, that salvation has been purchased, and that forgiveness is the birthright of every believing penitent. This is the plea of our prayer for sanctification, "for by one offering he hath perfected for ever them that are sanctified." This is the foundation of our plea for physical healing, for "Himself took our infirmities, and bare our sicknesses," and purchased redemption for our suffering bodies. And on this ground we may claim every other needed blessing, for "He that spared not his own Son, but delivered him up for us all, how shall he not with him also freely give us all things?"

Have we learned the meaning of His name and the power of His cross and blood as the strong and all-prevailing plea of the believing suppliant at the throne of grace?

"In his name," means, finally, in union and complete identity with Him. It expresses our relation to Him as well as His relation to the Father. It means in His person, in His stead, on His account, as if the petitioner were the very Son Himself. We all know something of how far a human name and introduction will go. The friend we introduce in our name is received, in some sense, as we would be received. Still more is this the case when he is commended to us on the ground of intimate relations with the one we love. The wife is received by her husband's family as if she were part of him and kin with them. In his name she comes to them as he would come. Sometimes we see this relationship very strongly and strangely illustrated in the case of those who otherwise would have no claim whatever for consideration.

In the days that followed the American war, many an incident was told of the tender bonds of fellowship and suffering, on the battlefield or in the Southern hospital— bonds which often gave the stranger a place in the old homestead as dear as that of the fallen soldier boy whom he had befriended. One such incident is related of a wretched tramp who called one day at a farmhouse in the west and was refused, very naturally, by the suspicious housewife. But the stranger drew from his well-worn pocket a scrap of paper and handed it to the woman. It was the writing of her boy, and it told how this man had fought by his side and then had nursed him in the hospital until the last hour had come; and how, as these lines were being written, he was committing his dying body and his last messages for home and mother to his hands; and it asked them, if they ever met, to receive him and love him as he had been loved and cherished, for his sake and in his name. That was enough. The haggard face and ragged dress and tramp-like appearance of the stranger were all forgotten, and the rough man was clasped in that mother's arms and taken to that home circle as a child, for the sake of another.

It is thus that we become identified with Jesus, and our Father receives us in His name as He receives Him. This is what faith may claim as it comes in His name. We enter into His rights, we ask on His account, and we expect to be welcomed and loved even as He is loved. This was His own bequest to us in His intercessory prayer in the seventeenth chapter of John, "That the world may know that thou hast . . . loved them, as thou hast loved me," and "that the love wherewith thou hast loved me may be in them, and I in them." Is it too bold if we claim that which He Himself has asked for us as our place of privilege and right?

Not only, however, may we claim His rights; we must also come in His will and spirit, and ask as He claims and only what He Himself would ask. The privilege is limited by its own very nature. We cannot ask in the behalf of Christ what Christ Himself would not ask if He were praying. "In his name," therefore, necessarily means in harmony with His will and at the prompting of His Spirit. We may not, therefore, claim from God that which would be sinful or selfish, or involve harm to another, or hindrance to the cause of Christ. All our asking must be within this eternal limit, "Thy will be done in earth, as it is in heaven." But this will is as large as the utmost of our being. Within this large and ample place there is room for every reasonable petition for spirit, soul, and body, family and friends, temporal circumstances, spiritual services, and utmost possibilities of human desire, hope or blessing.

And, finally, this identity with Him implies that He will be in us as the spirit of faith, making it His prayer and supplying the spirit and conditions of effectual prevailing intercession.

Such then, beloved, is the divinely appointed channel of prayer. Oh, how it encourages the unworthy and weak to come with full assurance of faith to the mercy seat! You may be a poor sinner, but He who represents you yonder is the Righteousness of God and bears upon His brow, above your name, the flashing jeweled coronet which inscribes your standing, "Holiness unto the Lord." You may be an obscure and insignificant disciple, but He who endorses your petition has the mightiest name in earth and heaven. You may be a timid spirit and a faint-hearted child of unbelief and fear, but He who bids you have the faith of God and Who offers Himself to you as the spirit of faith and prevailing prayer is the One who said on earth, "Father . . . I knew that thou hearest me always." "Father, I will that they also, whom thou hast given me, be with me where I am," and in His faith you may claim with boldness all His will, and go forth in deepest humility, but sublimest confidence, saying,

> I am not skilled to understand
>> What God hath willed, what God hath planned,
> But this I know, at His right hand,
>> Stands One who is my Savior.

~ 4 ~

The Prayer of Faith

"And Jesus answering saith unto them,
Have faith in God. For verily I say unto
you, That whosoever shall say unto this
mountain, Be thou removed, and be thou
cast into the sea; and shall not doubt in
his heart, but shall believe that those
things which he saith shall come to pass;
he shall have whatsoever he saith. Therefore I say unto you, What things soever
ye desire, when ye pray, believe that ye
receive them, and ye shall have them"
(Mark 11:22–24).

THERE IS an unseen principle of force in the material
world which is mightier far than all the physical elements that we touch and see. It is the force of attraction

which, in its twofold form of cohesion and gravitation, holds the physical universe together. As the force that condenses and holds in cohesion the minutest particles of matter, it is the cause by which, in a sense, all things consist or hang together. But for this cohesive force, our bodies would dissipate into impalpable air, the raindrops and the oceans would dissolve into vapor, the mighty mountains would crumble to pieces, and the great world itself would explode in a catastrophe of wreck and dissolution. And in its wider and far-reaching application, it is the force that holds our planet in its orbit and keeps it, on its awful journey of a thousand miles a minute and more than five hundred million miles a year, from rushing into the distant fields of immensity, or diverging a hair-breadth from its unmarked path amidst the spheres, or even quivering in its course notwithstanding the terrific velocity of its career. It is the same force that holds all the planets on their aerial track, and all the systems that circle round ten thousand suns in all their spheres, without collision or catastrophe. It is the mighty power of gravitation. All unseen it is, and noiseless. There is no vibration in its mighty heart-throbs; no reverberation from its voice; no trace of its viewless but mighty arm. Yet, it is mightier than the earth which it poises in space and propels along its pathway; mightier than the sun, from whose center it sweeps the circle of the solar system with its revolving circuit of planets; mightier than all the stars in all their spheres; the great, invisible, intangible, inaudible, impalpable secret of the material universe and all its mighty movements. How simple is this subtle force, and yet how sufficient and sublime!

But now let us ascend from the material world to the social, rational, and human sphere, and there, too, we shall find a corresponding principle which holds society together, even as the law of gravitation holds the worlds of space. What is that principle that binds the family together, that cements the friendships of life, that controls the partnerships of business, that forms the basis of commercial confidence and the greatest transactions of business, and leads men continually to stake their whole fortune and every material interest on their investments and securities? Why, it is simply confidence, trust, faith between man and man! Without it, the home circle would be torn with strife and wrecked with distrust and misery. Without it, political and national fabrics would collapse, and government would be impossible. Without it, business would be ruined. No single bank could stand a day without the trust of its constituents, and no security would be worth anything were men to cease to trust the promises and reliability of their fellow men. The world is adopting this very name of trust in this day for its strongest institutions. Everything now is taking the form of a commercial trust. There must be some fascination in the term, and well there may be, for it is the very cohesive principle of society, the law of gravitation for the whole social world.

Let us now carry this thought to its true plane and apply it to the great spiritual kingdom of which all natural things are but imperfect types. Should it seem strange if this law of faith were found to be the very principle of the spiritual world as it is of the natural, the underlying force which holds it together, and the remedial principle which is to bring back our own lost orb to its true place in the circle of the heavens? Such indeed it is. Faith is the essential principle of the Kingdom of God. It was the loss of faith which separated man from God in Eden. The fall of the race began the moment they listened to Satan's insinuations, "Hath God said?" And the recovery of the race commences the moment the soul begins to trust its God. This is why faith has been made indispensable to the reception of the gospel and the salvation of the soul. This is why it is forever true, "He that believeth on the Son hath everlasting life: and he that believeth not the Son shall not see life; but the wrath of God abideth on him." Faith is the gateway of salvation, and it is not strange that it should be made the gateway of prayer.

Let us consider this great subject thoughtfully and prayerfully, and may the Holy Spirit search our hearts on this solemn matter, until we shall be convicted of sin because we believe not. For this is the condemnation, because they have not believed on the name of the Son of God.

Faith is necessary in order to have acceptable and effectual prayer. This our Lord very distinctly states in this passage. He commands the disciples to have faith in God and then adds, "When ye pray, believe that ye receive them." But this is not the only place where this necessity is emphasized, for we are told in Hebrews that "without faith, it is impossible to please him: for he that cometh to God must believe that he is, and that he is the rewarder of them that diligently seek him." There must be a believing recognition of God's personal existence and of His goodness and graciousness, and that He does hear and answer prayer.

So, again, in speaking of prayer for healing, it is declared that "the prayer of faith shall save the sick, and the Lord shall raise him up." If we would understand what James means by the prayer of faith, we have only to turn to the first chapter and hear him say, "If any of you lack wisdom, let him ask of God, that giveth to all men liberally" (or rather, "of course"), "but let him ask in faith, nothing wavering. For he that wavereth is like a wave of the sea driven with the wind and tossed. For let not that man think that he shall receive anything of the Lord." The language here is very emphatic. "Of course" God will give to all, but they must take by faith what God gives, or the giving is in vain. The man who wavers does not take, cannot receive. He is like that poor victim in the hospital who died in agony with water held to his lips, but unable to swallow a single drop through the spasms which contracted his throat, arising from the most terrific of all human diseases. There are people to whom the

Lord gives the Water of Life, but they will not drink it. There are people whose tables God has spread with the blessings of faith, but they do not partake of its bounties. There are prayers which God has answered, but we do not enjoy the answers. There are souls whom God has long ago forgiven, but they are in darkness and despair because they did not trust His pardon. Therefore, when the troubled and despairing father came to Him about his child, crying, "I spake to thy disciples that they should cast him out; and they could not . . . but if thou canst do any thing, have compassion on us, and help us," the Master simply answered, as He turned the whole question back upon the man, "If thou canst believe, all things are possible to him that believeth."

It is perfectly right that God should require us to believe before He answers our prayers because faith is the law of the New Testament and the gospel dispensation. The Apostle Paul speaks of two laws in the third chapter of Romans: the law of works and the law of faith. The former has been superseded, and the principle on which the whole gospel is based is the law of faith. "To him that worketh not, but believeth on him that justifieth the ungodly, his faith is counted for righteousness." We have already suggested why this law has been adopted. No doubt in the light of eternity we shall find many reasons for it which we could not now fully apprehend, but it is enough to know that as it was through unbelief that men fell, so it is through faith that they must be restored.

In a word, we must come back to the point from which we started in a wrong direction. When Bunyan's pilgrim found that he had lost his roll on the Hill of Difficulty, he simply went back to the place where he had lost it and started on again. And so we must begin at the point of departure from God by learning to trust Him. God is bound to act upon this principle if it be the law of this dispensation, and He cannot justly acknowledge our plea if we do not present it according to the prescribed rule.

If this be true, it works most solemnly in both directions; and while, on one side, it is gloriously certain, "According to your faith be it unto you," yet, on the other, it may be just as true, "According to your unbelief it shall be unto you." It may be that God for very consistency is required to keep His word to those who doubt Him as well as to those who believe Him, and that the enemy of souls might even accuse Him of falsehood and inconsistency if He answered the prayer of unbelief. He has announced this as the principle of His throne of grace, the very law on which petitions will receive attention and consideration, and surely we cannot afford to disregard this sacred intimation or venture into His presence expecting our unbelieving complaint and insulting doubts and insincerities to bring any blessing from His hand.

But faith is not only the law of the Christian dispensation; it is also a mighty force in the spiritual world. We are touching now upon a subject which the wisest spirits can but dimly comprehend, but upon which, perhaps, there is light enough to be well assured that the very act of believing for anything which God has promised is an actual creative force and produces effects and operations of the most important character. Indeed it seems that faith is the very principle upon which God Himself acts, and the secret of His power in creating matter and in commanding the events of providence. "He spake, and it was done; he commanded, and it stood fast." When the disciples wondered at the withering of the fig tree, Jesus simply said it was an act of divine faith. It was the faith of God that produced it, and then He commanded them to "have faith in God." The faith of God must mean the faith which God Himself exercises. In the fourth chapter of Romans, we are told a little about this faith of God when it is said that Abraham acted like Him "who quickeneth the dead, and calleth those things which be not as though they were." He commands that which is not and expects it and believes in the efficacy of His own command without a shadow of hesitation, and He sees it instantly or ultimately accomplished. And even for the things that lie in the future in His purpose, He counts them as if they were present or past. The lapse of time is nothing in His mind and involves no uncertainty as to the results. He so believes in the things that are not that He calls them by the names of actual realities. He called Abraham "the father of many nations" before he even had a child, and made him call himself by the same significant name. He calls Jesus Christ "His only begotten Son," "the

Lamb slain before the foundation of the world," and the cross was as real to the Father ages ago as it is now. He speaks of you and me as if we were already sitting in the heavenly palaces in the ages to come and shining like the sun in the kingdom of our Father.

It was this faith in Jesus Christ that commanded and compelled the quickening of Lazarus in his tomb. It was a resistless force, a divine power that actually moved upon second causes and compelled their obedience; and if that faith of God be in us, it will be a corresponding force, and there shall be in us that effectual working prayer which availeth much, which, at the very moment we are offering it and believing for it, is moving something or upon some heart, and making someone conscious of the presence of the power of God.

Surely this is reason enough, then, that we should pray in faith. It is a spiritual force which God requires of us to cooperate with, to enter into, to use with Him and for His glory. The mighty forces of nature must have man's cooperation, or they are lost and wasted. The electricity goes to waste if we do not constrain it to our will and use it according to its own laws. And so God's omnipotence must be taken hold of by our faith and actually used, in deep humility but holy confidence, for the carrying through of His own great purposes. Could we see what is behind the curtains of the invisible world, we should be able to trace living streams of spiritual influence passing from the heavens at the very instant that the prayer of faith is ascending from some lonely closet, and terminating upon the very persons at that very instant whose names are being held up before the throne. Two streams of heavenly power would be distinctly visible: one an ascending line of prayer from the kneeling suppliant, and the other a descending current of power upon some far distant heart. Such phenomena have actually been traced in innumerable instances. While Elijah was praying on Carmel, the clouds were actually marshaling on the distant horizon; while Jacob was praying at Peniel, the heart of Esau, as he lay in his tent that night, was going back to early memories, and melting into the tender welcome which he gave at that noontide to his once-hated brother. While some of God's remembrancers have been holding up special fields in far distant lands, it has been actually found at that very moment showers of blessing have been descending on that special field prayed for. While some weeping wife or mother has been praying for her husband or boy, that husband or boy was being converted hundreds of miles away. Faith is therefore a force as mighty as that which we control when we touch the electric button, or open the valve of the engine, or pull the little cord that explodes the mighty subterranean battery which upheaves the mountain of rock or discharges the sunken torpedo. In requiring us, therefore, to pray in faith, God simply requires us to join hands with Himself in the exercise of His own almighty power, and be partakers of His mighty working.

The faith which God requires of us in prayer is essential to our own spiritual welfare; and, if it add no direct ulterior result in the actual answer, it would be abundantly repaid in the blessing which believing prayer brings to our own spirit. How it quiets our fears, tranquilizes our agitation, and stills our troubled spirit! How it enables us to submit to God and say, "Thy will be done," as we never can until we believe that His will for us is only love and blessing. Indeed, so wonderful are the subjective benefits of prayer that many go so far as to say that this is all the value of prayer. This would be a very foolish conclusion to adopt, for it would be a strange blessing if we were only comforted by an imaginary dream which had no objective reality. Take away the actual reality of God and the facts of prayer, and you take away the foundation of our subjective comfort; for, if God be not real and the answer not actual, why, our comfort is a lie, and our ulterior peace a delusive dream. But if we know God is real, and that His promise will be actually fulfilled, then indeed we can rest our troubled heads upon His breast and our hearts upon His promises, and be still and know that He is God.

How self-possessed and restful the hearts that have learned to trust God for all they ask! How sweetly these two thoughts are combined in the benignant words of the apostle in Philippians: "Be careful for nothing; but in everything by prayer and supplication with thanksgiving let your requests be made known unto God. And the peace of God, which passeth all understanding, shall keep your hearts and minds through Christ Jesus." There we have the injunction to pray about everything—the requirement to pray without care, doubt, or anxiety, and then the promise that the peace of God shall keep our hearts and minds through Jesus Christ.

But God requires our trust in order to keep us from hindering His answer to our prayer by our own restless activity or flight. When we ask God to do anything for us, we must give Him time to do it, and carefully avoid rushing off in unbelieving haste to do something that would probably quite hinder His plan. Many a time, if God were to come with the answer to our prayer, He would find that we were not there, but had simply run away in fear and doubt, first firing our gun like a sentinel, and then getting off as fast as our limbs could carry us. Suppose Israel had not believed God when they cried unto Him at the Red Sea, but had rushed back upon their foes or forward into the deep or away into the mountains, where God could never have answered their prayer by dividing the sea. To prevent this He had to say to them first, "Stand still, and see the salvation of the Lord," and then bid them go forward in His way and claim it.

If Joshua's hosts had not believed in God and marched around Jericho at His command, they never would have found the answer which was awaiting their seventh circuit on the seventh day. We find, in the thirtieth chapter of Isaiah, the prophet pleading with his people to be quiet and not hinder the deliverance which they had asked God to give them from Sennacherib and his army. But instead of this, they insisted upon doing something to help themselves: they sent an embassy into Egypt for an alliance with Pharaoh. The prophet warned them without avail that the Egyptians should help in vain, and that their strength was to sit still. "In quietness and in confidence shall be your strength; and ye would not. But ye said, No; for we will flee upon horses." And God answered, Get all the horses you want; you will need them soon, for "they that pursue you be swift." Then the prophet adds, "Therefore will the Lord wait, that he may be gracious unto you," for "blessed are all they that wait for him." In due time they found out their Egyptian alliance was a broken reed and a reed that pierced the hand that leaned upon it. The Egyptians were helpless, and Sennacherib, furious that they should have gone to Egypt, returned with a fierce and cruel scorn, and bade his caged prisoners prepare for their doom. Then they were shut up to faith and cried unto the Lord alone, and lo, in a moment, without any of their contriving, God sent an angel at night, who simply swept along the line of Syrian tents, shook his fiery wings above those slumbering hosts, and their vital breath ceased and the morning saw an army of corpses, and the caged and invested city found itself gloriously free!

So God requires us to trust Him and be still until He brings His answer to us and works it out in our lives, and

71

without faith we are sure to do something to hinder Him or get out of the place where we can receive the answer in its fullness.

It is reasonable to believe for an answer which we do not yet see. How can I believe for that which I do not know or see to be actually so? Simply because if you did see and know from other evidence, it would not be believing at all, but learning from the evidence of your senses. You only believe when you do not see. "Faith is the evidence of things not seen." God's way for us is to believe first, on the simple evidence of His promise, and to continue to believe without other evidence until we have proved our faith without sight; then He will permit us to see and know by the demonstration of the fact itself.

This is nothing more than we are doing every day in the affairs of human life. Millions of dollars are invested in our commercial exchanges every week on the simple faith of a telegram or an item of news in the daily papers. Values are bought and sold on paper where the actual realities have not been seen by either party. Securities are constantly negotiated by those who buy them on simple trust. Every time we send a telegram and act upon it, we are venturing on simple faith in the operator that despatches it, on the wire that carries it, and the messenger boy that delivers it. We do not see it go, nor do we see it received, but we rest, and probably take most important action on the certainty that it has gone and that the matter has been settled. It is surely very humiliating that we cannot put the same confidence in the Word of our God as we do in the fidelity of a messenger boy.

Then again, we are constantly in the habit of recognizing things as done when in fact they are only decided and long weeks and even months must intervene before we see the actual accomplishment. A friend of mine had an application for a pension before Congress. It meant everything to her and her helpless husband and family. On one side was a life of toil and suffering; on the other, comfort and happiness for those she loved better than her life. There was considerable delay and uncertainty, but at last the message was flashed across the wires from Washington one day, and she quickly hastened to tell me the glad news, with tears of joy. She said, "I have got my husband's pension, praise the Lord!" But if one of our critics had been there, I suppose he would have said, "Madam, you are telling a story; you have not a single dollar of your pension, and won't have a single dollar of it for months to come." And the critic, in one sense, would have been right, for she herself told me in the same breath, "It will be several months before we have it actually, for it has to go through a great deal of red tape, but that does not make any difference."

And so the dear woman went ahead in simple faith, and long before she had the money, all the arrangements for her future life were made as calmly and surely as if she had had the first installment deposited in the bank. To her, the decree of the supreme authority was enough; the question of time meant nothing, and she could truthfully say, even in the face of the critic, "I have my pension." Honestly and actually she did have all that was necessary to make it certain and to give her the benefit of it.

And so the moment our petition passes the Throne, we are justified in believing that we have just what we ask and in saying, like her, "I have got my answer, praise the Lord!" This was what God intended to teach Daniel when He sent the angel from heaven, after he had been praying twenty-one days, to say to him, "From the first day that thou didst set thine heart to understand, and to chasten thyself before thy God, thy words were heard, and I am come for thy words. But the prince of the kingdom of Persia withstood me one and twenty days." In the very beginning his prayer passed the Throne above, and he was justified all those three weeks in counting the answer given, but the delivery of the blessing and even the message was hindered by the opposition of the enemy. But all the opposition of earth or hell cannot hinder God's purposes, and to His mind and the mind of faith, they are as certain from the beginning as after they have taken form like the solid mountains and become the facts and memories of actual life.

Indeed, all God's promises to His children are gauged on this pattern. To the penitent sinner, Christ's word was instant and final: "Thy faith hath saved thee." To the disciples His message of cleansing was, "Now ye are clean through the word which I have spoken unto you."

To the sick and suffering the decree always went forth, "Be thou clean," "Receive thy sight," "Be it unto thee even as thou wilt," "Thy son liveth," "According to thy faith be it unto thee." To Abraham the promise that carried with it all the promises of the future was in the perfect tense, "I have made thee the father of many nations." And the explanation given was that God, as the very principle of His government, "calleth those things which be not as though they were." This very thing that so many shrink from is the very essence of all true faith, and the lack of it teaches the very line of demarcation between effectual faith and that which is only hope.

Shall we then, beloved, recognize the reasonableness of faith and rise to something higher than the mere reasonings of probability and the mere hope and encouragements to which men can rise without the need of God at all? Shall we count God's Word more true than all our evidences and feelings, than all the endorsements of men, than all the actual evidences of its fulfillment, for even the latter may not be abiding, but "the word of God abideth forever," and "one jot or one tittle shall in no wise pass from the law, till all be fulfilled.

Let us learn to be very deliberate in our prayers. Many persons pour out a reckless mass of ill-considered supplication very much as a boy blows his soap bubbles into the air, scarcely expecting ever to see them again. It is doubtful if such persons go through the mental effort of believing or attempting to believe that they shall surely receive one in ten of these petitions. Certainly, if they should receive them, it would take a very busy life to hold all the answers and turn them to practical account. The habit of asking indiscriminately wears out the very power of believing. It is a pity ever to ask anything from God which we have to abandon or confess to be of no significance. It is a very serious thing to take the name of our God in vain, and everything asked in His name without meaning or effect is of this character. Every time we find our prayers ineffectual, we are weakened for our next attempt, and after a time, like iron heated and cooled successively, the temper of our faith is worn out and its very fiber disintegrated like the rusty metal. If we would ever learn the prayer of faith, we must learn to pray with thoughtful deliberation and carefully weigh our words before the Lord as He has weighed His promises, for "the words of the Lord are as silver tried in a furnace." The secret of faith is always to endeavor to ascertain, before we ask, whether we are asking according to His will, and then to take the simple stand of John the beloved: "If we ask anything according to his will, he heareth us: and if we know that he hear us, whatsoever we ask, we know that we have the petitions that we desired of him."

Let us cultivate the habit of definitely believing when we have thus prayed. Let us commit the matter to God and recognize it henceforth as one of the things He has promised and passed, and a thing for which we cannot pray again in the sense of an unsettled question. Faith is a matter of definite will, to a certain extent at least. We must choose to believe and fix our will as the sailor sets his helm; then God will swell our sails and hold our helm for us in the attitude in which we set it. We cannot create the faith, but we can choose to believe, and God will sustain us in our choice and uphold us in our trust.

We must claim the faith of God, the Spirit of Jesus, the enabling of His trust, to sustain ours. We choose to believe, but He must enable us to claim even His own promises. This follows, of course, consistently with the whole doctrine of Christ's indwelling life. We must trust Him for our faith as well as for our love and holiness, but in each case we must yield ourselves and choose to stand in the position assumed, and then throw ourselves upon Him to sustain us. This He will do, baptizing us with such a spirit of prayer and confidence that we shall be enabled to claim and humbly command the blessing which He has already decreed.

And then we must stand fast, and not be shaken by either delay or apparent denial, drawing comfort and encouragement even from His seeming refusals, until at last our Lord shall look upon us as He did the Syro-Phoenician woman, with admiring love, and say: "Great is thy faith: be it unto thee even as thou wilt."

Beloved, let us realize that God is educating us for higher destinies, and placing upon us, day by day, heavier loads of discipline, that we may be thus trained for the mightier activities of faith, which, in the eternal world, we are to share with our enthroned Lord. Let us not stagger under these loads, but, like Abraham of old, be "strong in faith, giving glory to God; and being fully persuaded that, what he had promised, he was able also to perform," and we shall find that "our light affliction, which is but for a moment," has worked out for us "a far more exceeding and eternal weight of glory."

∾ 5 ∾

Hindrances to Prayer

"That your prayers be not hindered" (1 Peter 3:7).

THE GREATEST HINDRANCE to the life of prayer is sin. "The Lord's hand is not shortened, that it cannot save; neither his ear heavy, that it cannot hear: but your iniquities have separated between you and your God, and your sins have hid his face from you, that he will not hear." God would rather let Israel be defeated at Ai and go into captivity to Babylon, notwithstanding the prayers of Joshua in the one case, or even Noah, Daniel, and Job, if they could have interceded, in the other, so long as the answering of these prayers would have countenanced the sin of His people. Yes, even that beautiful and consecrated temple must be consumed to ashes and the very name of Jehovah dishonored by His enemies, rather than sin in the slightest degree be sanctioned by a holy God.

"If I regard iniquity in my heart, the Lord will not hear me." Even the cherished purpose of sin will thus hinder our prayers. The Apostle John most clearly adds his testimony to this heart-searching truth when he tells us: "If our heart condemn us, God is greater than our heart, and knoweth all things. If our heart condemn us not, then have we confidence toward God. And whatsoever we ask, we receive of him, because we keep his commandments, and do those things that are pleasing in his sight."

The old farmer, who tried to get peace at the altar by the prayers of the saints, was quite right when he told them one night that the Lord would never answer their prayers "so long as that ox was in the wrong stall." He hurried away to return his neighbor's property and came back the next night with shining face and light heart to testify to the blessing that came the moment he put the hindrance away.

God can hear the prayers of sinners, or else none of us could have access to the throne of grace, but this is a different matter from expecting Him to answer our prayers while we are deliberately committing sin without an honest purpose to abstain from it. This is the coolest insolence and presumption in the face of heaven. The sin may be confessed and put away, and the Lord will freely bless; but while we stand with evil conscience and wrong intent and expect God to countenance our disobedience and presumption, we can only accept the awful message which He gave to the leaders of Israel in the fourteenth chapter of Ezekiel: "Son of man, these men have set up their idols in their heart, and put the stumbling block of their iniquity before their face: should I be enquired of at all by them? Therefore speak unto them, and say unto them, Thus saith the Lord God: Every man of the house of Israel that setteth up his idols in his heart, and putteth the stumbling block of his iniquity before his face, and cometh to the prophet; I the Lord will answer him that cometh according to the multitude of his idols. . . . For everyone of the house of Israel, or of the stranger that sojourneth in Israel, which separateth himself from me, and setteth up his idols in his heart, and putteth the stumbling block of his iniquity before his face, and cometh to a prophet to enquire of him concerning me, I the Lord will answer him by myself: and I will set my face against that man, and will make him a sign and a proverb, and I will cut him off from the midst of my people; and ye shall know that I am the Lord."

This will frequently be found to be the cause of long-unanswered prayers and the failure of God's people to enter into the fullness of the blessing they are seeking. God is searching their hearts and bringing to their remembrance long-forgotten sins with which He wants them to deal thoroughly. Hence, when we are at some secret crisis of life, seeking, perhaps, entire sanctification, the baptism of the Holy Spirit, the healing of some critical and alarming disease, the life of some precious friend, or deliverance in some great emergency, God searches

the heart as with eyes of flame, and brings to our conscience things long buried in oblivion, and enables us to
search and try our ways and lay open all our heart before
Him. Then we may receive His blessing unhindered and
unbounded and know the blessedness of the man "whose
transgression is forgiven, whose sin is covered . . . and in
whose spirit there is no guile."

Beloved, let us search and try our ways, and turn
again unto the Lord. Let us be willing to say, "Search me,
O God, and know my heart; try me and know my ways,
and see if there be any wicked way in me, and lead me in
the way everlasting." Let us bring every Achan to the light
and to the sentence of death, and we shall find that even
sin cannot hinder our prayers nor our perfect blessing if
it is truly put away, but the valley of Achor will become
the very door of hope, and the place of forgiven sin and
self-crucifixion will be marked as the starting point of a
new and higher life of usefulness.

Another hindrance to prayer is selfishness and earthly
desire. "Ye ask, and receive not," says the Apostle James,
"because ye ask amiss, that ye may consume it upon your
lusts." God cannot give us all the things that our carnal
nature clamors for any more than we would give our child
the gleaming razor for which its little hands reach out in
such eager desire. They would often be more hurtful to us
than the keen edge of the steel to the thoughtless child.
Many a good thing may be desired from an earthly and
selfish motive and in a carnal spirit. Many a person seeks

forgiveness to escape the remorse of a guilty conscience and that he may be at ease to go on again in a life of godless selfishness. Most people, who have no true sense of honor, are quite willing to be accepted as candidates for heaven if God will let them enjoy the pleasures of the world on their way. Prayer for healing may be simply the expression of the desire to get free from pain and be able to enjoy the pleasures of life. Even Simon Magus wanted the power of the Holy Spirit from a thoroughly base and unholy motive. Things that God in other circumstances would be quite willing to give us, He has often to refuse us as they would really separate us from Him. At a later period of our lives we find Him able and willing to give us the same things without reserve because, in the meanwhile, we have been able to lay them all on His altar, to be used to His glory and in union with Himself.

Therefore, the Lord's Prayer, as we have already seen, begins with the prostration of our whole being at the feet of God and the threefold consecrating prayer, "Hallowed be thy name, thy kingdom come, thy will be done." We cannot be trusted to ask anything for ourselves until our spirit is thus consecrated to God.

This is the meaning of that profound promise in the thirty-seventh Psalm, "Delight thyself also in the Lord; and he shall give thee the desires of thine heart." The heart that has found its joy in God cannot desire anything that God cannot grant. He gives it first its desires and then their fulfillment.

Beloved, have not many of your unanswered prayers been thoroughly selfish ones? Have not your very longings for your own spiritual good been prompted either by a slavish fear or a narrow self-love? Have not your prayers for the salvation of your children and friends been as selfish as your desire to see them well settled in life, and perhaps you have never once offered a petition for anyone else's child or made an effort to bring them to Christ? It is all right that we should seek these blessings for ourselves and for our own, but if it be a true spirit of prayer and union with God, there will be something higher than mere selfish or human love or desire.

An insuperable barrier to unanswered prayer is the spirit of strife and bitterness. "When ye stand praying," our Savior said to His disciples, "forgive, if ye have ought against any." "Let none of you imagine evil in your hearts against his neighbor," is the message of the prophet Zechariah to the people of the Restoration, as he teaches them the secret of God's blessing in their critical trials. Job had to pray for his very enemies and banish from his heart every particle of bitter feeling toward the men who had tormented him through months of sickness with their ignorance, misconstruction, and offensive interference, before God turned his captivity and restored him to more than his former blessings. One reason why the disciples could not claim the casting out of the demon from the suffering child was that they had disputed by the way which should be the greatest. The spirit of cherished animosity, lurking prejudice, sullen vindictiveness, or cold disdain will as effectively obstruct our intercourse and intimacy with heaven as a speck upon the crystalline lens of the eye will obstruct our vision, or the crossing of the wires of the electric machinery of a building will leave us in darkness.

There are a great many crossed wires in the church of Christ, and the consequence is dark hearts and mournful cries: "Hath God forgotten to be gracious?" "How long, O Lord, wilt thou not hear my prayer?" Just this long, brother: "If thou bring thy gift to the altar, and there rememberest that thy brother hath ought against thee; leave there thy gift before the altar, and go thy way; first be reconciled to thy brother, and then come and offer thy gift."

The spirit of prayer is essentially a spirit of love. Frequently when we are at some crisis of prayer and very much is hanging upon God's answer, perhaps life itself, or something more precious than life, we shall find ourselves confronted with just such a test as this. Someone will be thrown across our path where all the strength of the natural heart, with its dislikes, prejudices, and self-wills, will be laid hold of by the enemy to hinder our victory. Oh, let us remember at such an hour that we cannot hurt another by our irritation or retaliation, but we can deeply wound ourselves and hinder the blessing of our God! In the presence of Infinite Love, no breath of hate can live one moment. The simple lines of the old English poet are sweetly true:

He prayeth best who loveth best,
  All things both great or small,
For the great God who loveth us,
  He made and loveth all.

It is especially with respect to this matter of love that the Apostle John speaks of our heart condemning us in prayer, and above all other things it is perhaps that which we are most likely to overlook and God is least likely to pass by. "The greatest thing in the world," as Professor Drummond so happily styles it, "is love, and it is the one business of life to learn it."

Beloved, is this hindering your prayers? Can you think this moment of some brother or sister from whom you are wrongly estranged; some person whom you treat with studied harshness, neglect, perhaps disdain, or possibly with injury and injustice; some word that you have spoken against your brother, and which you should not have spoken even if true; some word to which you have listened against your brother, and never should have heard except in his presence, some cherished suspicion, criticism, or judgment where you have no business even to think evil? May God help you to see the way to discover some cause of unanswered prayer!

The habit of doubt is a hindrance to prayer. "He that wavereth is like a wave of the sea driven with the wind and tossed. For let not that man think that he shall receive any thing of the Lord." This is strong language, but there is no doubt that the sin of unbelief, according to the divine standpoint, is the most hurtful of all spiritual conditions. It destroys the very contact of the soul with God as effectually as the cutting of a telegraph wire would prevent the transmission of a message. We have already seen that the word "receive" in this passage of James means take, and that it denotes not so much God's anger with the unbelief—for He does "give liberally and upbraideth not"—but it refers to the inability of the man to take what God gives. His doubt shuts up his whole spiritual sensibilities and capacities, and renders him incapable of absorbing and appropriating the blessing which is offered him at the time. God holds us responsible for our doubt but does not require us to produce, by our own will, the faith which brings us into contact with His love and blessing, for this is His impartation; but He does require us to prevent it from running out, as from leaking vessels, through all the openings of our miserable doubts. There is one thing that we can all do: we can refuse to doubt; we can refuse to entertain the questioning and fear, the morbid apprehension and subtle Satanic insinuation; and if we do this, God will do the rest and enable us to stand fast in faith, and press forward to the fullness of His blessing.

This is where the enemy concentrates his strongest attacks, waiting when the hour of trial comes and our prayer seems to be refused and delayed, and hurling all his shafts of fire and evil suggestion into our trembling hearts to try to drive us from our confidence and get us to betray our own cause by consenting to his wicked questionings. Therefore Christ has said, "Whosoever shall say unto this mountain, Be thou removed, and be thou cast into the sea; and shall not doubt in his heart . . . he shall have whatsoever he saith." So "Abraham staggered not at the promise of God through unbelief; but was strong in faith, giving glory to God." So we are to hold fast the faith we have professed without wavering, for, "He is faithful that promised." "Now the just shall live by faith: but if any man draw back, my soul shall have no pleasure in him." God waits to give His blessing to the soldiers who stand their ground and who, when the blessing comes, are there to claim it.

But perhaps you say, "I have already doubted, and forfeited my blessing. Is it then too late to receive the answer?" No, not if you will repent of your doubt as you would of any other sin, and immediately bring forth fruits meet for repentance by refusing from henceforth and forevermore to be betrayed into the same sin. Often we shall find that such a fall becomes the occasion of thoroughly convincing us of the sin of doubting and curing us of it forever.

Beloved, have you been trifling with God in this matter of prayer and defrauding yourself of the blessings for which you have already suffered so much? May the Lord set your face this day like a flint, and fix your feet on the rock and stay your soul upon God!

Our prayers will be hindered if we stand on forbidden ground, or in anything hold back from the Master's will. It is not necessary that there should be willful sin or actual vice and transgression of moral law. It may simply be disobedience to the Spirit's voice in some definite leading to service or testimony. We have known many instances of persons who did not receive the full answers to their prayers for the baptism of the Holy Spirit until they had definitely obeyed the voice of God in some particular where they had been shrinking or hesitating. We have known many sad cases of persons who have failed to receive the answer to their prayer for healing because they were standing in some forbidden place, holding back their testimony for God from timidity or the fear of man, or failing to take some step of faith to which the Holy Spirit was calling; and it was not until after months or even years of striving with God and bitter sorrow that they learned the lesson, and in prompt and thorough obedience received perfect deliverance and wondrous blessing.

The Bible has some very solemn instances of good men standing on forbidden ground and finding their power and defense departing from them. The mighty Samson lost all his hold upon God the moment he left his place of separation. Abraham had no power while in a compromising attitude in Egypt. Jacob had no vision of God during the years of his wandering. And even the good Josiah lost his heavenly protection and sacrificed his precious life because he stepped beyond the divine will and went unbidden against Pharaoh Necho, king of Egypt, who warned him of his fate if he persisted in his rash presumption. There is not one of us who stands on consecrated ground but would probably lose even life itself if we persisted in disobeying the distinct call of God to special service or pressing forward where He had said, "No."

It is a very solemn thing for those who are walking in the Spirit to trifle with His voice or be disobedient to His least command. Such disobedience may interrupt all intercourse and hinder all prayer.

But again, forbidden means may effectually interrupt our Father's blessing. It is possible to ask God's help in a proper manner and spirit, and then immediately go to work to help Him to fulfill our prayer in an unlawful manner. No doubt Jacob sincerely asked God for the coveted blessing, but he proceeded afterward to take the most unworthy means to accomplish his purpose, and involved himself in years of waiting and sorrow. No doubt Moses sincerely asked God to deliver Israel by His hand when forty years of age, but he proceeded in the most rash and improper manner to accomplish his patriotic desire by slaying an Egyptian, and involving himself in crime and peril from the hand of the king. Doubtless, Abraham thought that his compromise about Hagar was going to assist God in fulfilling His own promise of a son, but he only silenced the heavenly voice for many years and

brought upon himself domestic strife and trouble, hindering the object he had at heart. No doubt Saul of Tarsus
sincerely prayed for salvation for many a year, but he
sought it by his own righteousness and missed his aim by
not submitting himself to the righteousness of God, and
his whole race today are praying in vain for mercy, which
they reject by rejecting God's only appointed way.

Many a soul prays for sanctification but fails to enter
into the blessing because he does not intelligently understand and believingly accept God's appointed means
by Jesus Christ and the indwelling of the Spirit. Many
a prayer for the salvation of others is hindered because
the very friend who prays for his friend takes the wrong
course to bring about the answer and resorts to means
which are wholly fitted to defeat his worthy object. We
know many a wife who is pleading for her husband's soul
and hoping to win him by avoiding anything that may
offend him, yielding to all his worldly tastes in the vain
hope of attracting him to Christ. Far more effective would
be an attitude of fidelity to God and fearless testimony to
Him, such as God could bless. Many a church asks the
Lord for His blessing and then goes to work to defeat
it by methods of worldly conformity, which God never
can countenance. Many a congregation wonders why
it is so poor and struggling and its prayer for financial
resources never answered, and yet it may be found that
its financial methods are wholly unscriptural and often
unworthy of ordinary self-respect, and such as a decent

worldly institution would not stoop to depend upon. When we ask God for any blessing, we must allow Him to direct the steps which are to bring the answer. God will give His power to every heart that will let Him hold the reins. Many an invalid is praying for healing and yet directly neglecting God's very prescription for disease and resorting to means which He has not countenanced, and which probably He would utterly forbid, especially to one who claimed to be in the attitude of simple faith. God's answer must be brought by His own messengers, and the steps which we take in bringing about the answer must be based on His absolute direction.

Take, for example, the course of David the second time the Philistines invaded his realm after his coronation. Suppose David had done just what he had done before and marched directly against them and then asked God to bless him. He would have been defeated, for this time the command was entirely different from the previous occasion. "Thou shalt not go up; but fetch a compass behind them"—that is, take a circuitous course, march away from them first, then around by a flank movement—"and come upon them over against the mulberry trees. And let it be, when thou hearest the sound of a going in the tops of the mulberry trees, that then thou shalt bestir thyself: for then shall the Lord go out before thee, to smite the host of the Philistines." Here we see that the answer was dependent on explicit obedience to the Lord's directions.

Is this not the reason, beloved, of many of our unanswered prayers? Have we waited for our Master's orders and sought the answer in the direction that He bade? Oh, how solemn are the words of the prophet Zechariah respecting one of God's most precious promises, "This shall come to pass if ye diligently obey the voice of the Lord your God." And that is but the echo of God's word concerning Abraham, "I know him, that he will command his children and his household after him, and they shall keep the way of the Lord, to do justice and judgment; that the Lord may bring upon Abraham that which he hath spoken of him."

Perhaps the greatest hindrance to effectual prayer, and no doubt to the life of prayer, is ignorance respecting the Holy Spirit and the interior life. With so many, prayer is the hasty utterance of the mere natural heart. It is little more than the cry of a suffering brute or the wail of an almost unconscious babe. True, God hears the faithless cry of human misery, but this is not prayer. The voice which always reaches the Father's ear is the voice of a trusting child and the Holy Spirit breathing in the heart of that child. True prayer should be His prompting, and it is because most persons know Him so little, and walk with Him at such a distance, that they are comparative strangers to the language of heavenly communion.

The life of prayer is an interior life, a spiritual life, and many persons do not know this, and do not want it. It holds too constant a check upon the heart, it requires

93

too utterly that we should walk softly with our God. Most persons like to be their own masters, and the habit of walking step by step with God and submitting every thought and desire to an inward Monitor is intolerable to their imperious self-will, or at least unfamiliar to their experience.

But this is truly the very element of the life of prayer. It is an interior life. Its home is "the secret place of the most High," and its dwelling, "the shadow of the Almighty." It is the intercourse of an inseparable divine companionship. It is Enoch walking with God. It is Elisha clinging to his master and saying, "As the Lord liveth and as thy soul liveth, I will not leave thee." It is the very breathing of the inner man, and is as necessary and unintermittent as the pulsation of a human heart and the respiration of a human bosom.

Beloved, is not this the difficulty, after all, about your prayers? Are they not the spasmodic cries of great emergencies rather than the habitual intercourse of a heavenly life? If you were accustomed to walk ever by His side, you would not get so far that you need to call so loudly and so long in the hour of extremity. It is the habit of constant prayer that prepares us for the great conflicts of prayer, and he who in this neglects the moment will find himself unprepared for the emergencies. God is calling you to a closer walk with Him, to open your heart for His continual abiding, and to receive into your breast the Spirit of grace and supplications to become to you the

Mighty Advocate who shall inspire all your petitions and bear them on the strong wings of His love and power to the Advocate on high, through Whom you shall receive the answer of that Father who ever answers the prayer which He inspires.

We sometimes see it advertised by our great financial houses that they have a private wire with all the great centers of trade. He who possesses in his heart the Holy Spirit has a private wire to the throne, and at any moment can open and maintain direct communication with heaven and bring all its legions, if need be, to His immediate aid. O beloved, surely it is worth your while to yield yourself to a consecrated life and to allow your loving Lord to make your heart His temple and His throne, where prayer shall ever be the familiar and unbroken intercourse of a happy child with the Father Who is ever at hand.

Oh, how happy they who are thus within continual reach of the supply of every need and the balm for every wound! Sorrow may overshadow, Satan may assail, difficulty may encompass on every side, but, through prayer, relief is always new, and the victorious spirit returns fresh from every conflict with a strength, which, Phoenix-like, rises from its own ashes and grows with each renewing in freshness and gladness.

A South American traveler tells of a curious conflict which he once witnessed between a little quadruped and a terrific and poisonous snake of great size. The little creature seemed no match for its antagonist that threatened to destroy it and its helpless brood by a blow, but it fearlessly faced its mighty enemy and, rushing in its face, struck him with a succession of fierce and telling blows, but received at the onset a deep and apparently fatal wound from his poisonous fangs, which flashed for a moment with an angry fire, and then fastened themselves deep into the flesh of the daring little assailant. For a moment it seemed as if all was over, but the wise little creature immediately retired into the forest and, hastening to the plantain tree, eagerly devoured a portion of its leaves and immediately came back, apparently fresh and restored, to renew the fray with fresh vigor and determination. Again and again this strange spectacle was repeated; the serpent ferociously attacked, greatly exhausted, and again and again wounded its antagonist to death, as it seemed, but the little creature successively repaired to its simple prescription and returned to renewed victory, until, in the course of an hour or two, the battle was over, the mammoth reptile lay still and dead, and the little victor was unharmed in the midst of the nest and the helpless little ones, who had been thus saved from destruction.

How often we are wounded by the dragon's sting, wounded it would seem to death; and if we had to go through some long ceremony to reach the source of life, we must faint and die! But, blessed be His Name, there is ever, for us, a Plant of healing as near at hand as that which the forest holds in its shade, to which we may continually repair and come back refreshed, invigorated, transfigured, like Him, Who, as He prayed on the mount, shone with the brightness of celestial light; and, as He prayed in the garden, arose triumphant over the fear of death and strengthened from on high to accomplish the mighty battle of our redemption.

Oh, the victories of prayer! They are the mountain tops of the Bible. They take us back to the plains of Mamre, to the fords of Peniel, to the prison of Joseph, to the triumphs of Moses, to the victories of Joshua, to the deliverances of David, to the miracles of Elijah and Elisha, to the whole story of the Master's life, to the secret of Pentecost, to the keynote of Paul's unparalleled ministry, to the lives of saints and the deaths of martyrs, to all that is most sacred and sweet in the history of the Church and the experience of the children of God. And when, for us, the last conflict shall have passed, and the footstool of prayer shall have given place to the harp of praise, the scenes of time that shall be gilded with eternal radiance shall be those often linked with deepest sorrow and darkest night, over which we have written the inscription, "JEHOVAH-SHAMMA: The Lord was there!" Only that which God touched shall be remembered or worth remembering forever. These are imperishable memorials. Oh, that henceforth they may cover every pathway and every step of life's journey, and that we may recognize whatever comes as but another call to prayer and another opportunity for God to manifest His glory and erect the everlasting memorial of His victorious love!

We close this little message with the thought with which we began its first chapter—namely, that the way the Master taught His disciples to pray was by starting them at once to pray.

Begin this moment to pray for the very first thing that comes to your heart as a need, and go right on turning everything into prayer until you have to stop in the very fullness of your heart and turn it all into praise. And "now unto him that is able to do exceeding abundantly above all that we ask or think, according to the power that worketh in us, unto him be glory in the church by Christ Jesus throughout all ages, world without end. Amen."

THE POWER OF STILLNESS

The Power of Stillness

IT WAS "a still small voice," or the sound of a gentle stillness. Is there any note of music in all the chorus as mighty as the emphatic pause? Is there any word in all the Psalter more eloquent than the one word, "Selah" (Pause)? Is there anything more thrilling and awful than the hush that comes before the bursting of the tempest and the strange quiet that seems to fall upon all nature before some preternatural phenomenon or convulsion? Is there anything that can so touch our hearts as the power of stillness?

Sweet Stillness

THE SWEETEST BLESSING that Christ brings us is the Sabbath rest of soul, of which the Sabbath of creation was the type. There is, for the heart that will cease for itself, "the peace of God that passeth all understanding"—a quietness and confidence which is the source of all strength; a sweet peace "which nothing can offend." There is, in the deepest center of the believer's soul, a chamber of peace where God dwells, and where, if we will only enter in and hush every other sound, we can hear His "still voice."

A score of years ago, a friend placed in my hands a little book, which became one of the turning points of my life. It was called *True Peace* and was an old medieval message. It had but one thought, and it was this—that God was waiting in the depths of my being to talk to me if I would only get still enough to hear His voice

Stillness Challenged

I THOUGHT this would be a very easy matter, and so I began to get still. But I had no sooner commenced than a pandemonium of voices reached my ears, a thousand clamoring notes from without and within, until I could hear nothing but there noise and din. Some of them were my own questions, some of them my own cares, and some were my very prayers. Others were the suggestions of the tempter and the voices from the world's turmoil. Never before did there seem so many things to be done, to be said, to be thought. In every direction I was pushed and pulled and greeted with noisy acclamations and unspeakable unrest. It seemed necessary for me to listen to some of them and to answer; but God said, "Be still, and know that I am God."

The God of Stillness

THEN came the conflict of thoughts for the morrow, with its duties and cares. But God said, "Be still." And as I listened, and slowly learned to obey, and shut my ears to every sound, I found after a while, that when the other voices ceased, or I ceased to hear and heed them, there was a still, small voice in the depths of my being that began to speak with an inexpressible tenderness, power, and comfort. As I listened it became to me the voice of prayer, and the voice of wisdom, and the voice of duty, and I did not need to think so hard, but that "still, small voice" of the Holy Spirit in my heart was God's prayer in my secret soul; was God's answer to all my questions; was God's life and strength for soul and body, and became the substance of all knowledge, and all prayer, and all blessing; for it was the living GOD Himself as my life and my all.

We cannot go through life strong and fresh on constant express trains, with ten minutes for lunch; but we must have quiet hours, secret places of the Most High, times of waiting upon the Lord, when we renew our strength and learn to mount up on wings as eagles, and then come back to run and not be weary, and to walk and not faint.

The Way of Stillness

THE BEST THING about this stillness is that it gives God a chance to work. "He that entered into His rest hath ceased from his own works, even as God did from His." When we cease from our works, God works in us; when we cease from our thoughts, God's thoughts come into us; when we get still from our restless activities, "God worketh in us both to will and to do his good pleasure," and we have but to work it out.

Beloved! Let us take His stillness; let us dwell in "the secret place of the Most High"; let us enter into God and His eternal rest; let us silence the other sounds, and then we can hear "the still, small voice."

Then there is another kind of stillness: the stillness that lets God work for us, and we hold our peace; the stillness that ceases from controversy, and self-indication, and expedients of wisdom and forethought, and lets God provide and answer the unkind word and the cruel blow in His own unfailing, faithful love. How often we lose God's interposition by taking up our own cause and striking for our own defense.

There is no spectacle in all the Bible so sublime as the silent Savior answering not a word to the men that were maligning Him, and whom He could of laid prostrate at His feet by one look of Divine power, or one word of fiery rebuke. But he let them do their worst and He stood in the power of stillness—God's Holy Lamb.

God give to us this silent power, this mighty self-surrender, this conquered spirit, which will make us "more than conquerors through Him that loved us." Let our voice and our life speak like "the still, small voice" of Horeb, and as the "sound of gentile stillness." Then after the heat and strife of earth are over, men will remember the morning dew, the mellow light and sunshine, the evening breeze, the Lamb of Calvary, and the gentle, Holy, Heavenly Dove.

Made in the USA
Coppell, TX
11 June 2021